IMAGES
of America

THEATRES
OF HAWAI'I

10·18

This broadside, in English and Hawaiian, is from the Royal Hawaiian Theatre performances on December 18 and 20, 1880, of *Babes in the Woods*, a musical burlesque in three acts. This was a form of musical theatre with girls, gags, satire, and slang. The company's business manager and stage manager also doubled as performers.

ON THE COVER: The huge Hawai'i Theatre marquee, with the largest neon display in the islands, is ablaze for *Phantom Raiders*, July 28–30, 1940. This elaborate marquee was installed in 1938 and replaced the earlier, simple canopy and small readerboard listing the show. The vertical sign was put in when the theatre opened in 1922 and originally lit by electric bulbs, as neon signs were not introduced in Hawai'i until 1929. (Author's collection.)

IMAGES
of America

THEATRES
OF HAWAI'I

Lowell Angell

ARCADIA
PUBLISHING

Published by Arcadia Publishing
Charleston, South Carolina

Library of Congress Control Number: 2010932076

For all general information, please contact Arcadia Publishing:
Telephone 843-853-2070
Fax 843-853-0044
E-mail sales@arcadiapublishing.com
For customer service and orders:
Toll-Free 1-888-313-2665

Visit us on the Internet at www.arcadiapublishing.com

A theatre is a unique place; it has a "soul" filled with the dreams of its designers and builders, the dedication of those on stage or screen, and the emotions of millions who have sat in the darkness and experienced its offerings. This book is for all who enjoy historic theatres and especially those who strive to preserve their rich legacy for future generations.

CONTENTS

ACKNOWLEDGMENTS

I am grateful to many who helped make this book a reality:

Richard Sklenar, executive director, and staff and volunteers of the Theatre Historical Society of America, Elmhurst, Illinois (www.historictheatres.org). This national membership organization, founded in 1969, houses a rich and incomparable archive on more than 15,000 theatres and publishes an illustrated quarterly journal, *Marquee*.

Desoto Brown and the staff of Bishop Museum Archives. Thanks also to fellow historian Desoto for material from his extensive personal collection.

Roger Angell, my brother, for his photographs of longtime organist Johnny DeMello and Hilo theatres.

Bob Alder, former Waikiki Theatre organist, for his invaluable assistance with Big Island theatres.

Others who have been very helpful include Sarah Richards, Elaine Evans and Burton White, Hawai'i Theatre Center; Ross Stephenson, State Historic Preservation Office; Professor Bill Chapman, University of Hawai'i Historic Preservation Program; Kiersten Faulkner and the staff of Historic Hawai'i Foundation; Barbara Dunn, Hawaiian Historical Society; Susan Shaner and the staff of Hawai'i State Archives; Wesley Inouye, Pacific Theatres; Kylee Omo and Sara Lloyd, Punahou School Archive; Holly Buland, Alexander and Baldwin Sugar Museum; Kathleen Ramsden, Army Tropic Lightning Museum; Jeff Dodge AIA, historical architect, U.S. Navy; Jim Cartwright, University of Hawai'i archivist; Dore Minatodani, Hamilton Library, University of Hawai'i at Manoa; Bob Sigall, author of *The Companies We Keep*; Consolidated Amusement Company; Carol White, Mission Houses Museum Library; Libby Burke, Lyman Museum and Mission House; Richard Harger, Tom DeLay, Scott Bosch, Steve Fredrick, and fellow theatre historians and Arcadia authors, Mike Hauser, Jack Tillmany, and Gary Lee Parks.

And finally, Arcadia editor Debbie Seracini, whose calm demeanor and enthusiasm were both inspiring and appreciated.

The credit for my lifelong interest in theatres belongs to my mother and two aunts, who piqued my youthful imagination and curiosity with their recollections of dancing on the Hawai'i and Princess theatre stages as young girls in the 1920s.

I'm grateful to the many individuals who related their memories of theatres in Hawai'i. Anyone willing to share their stories, photos, or memorabilia is invited to contact me at theatresofhawaii@mail.com.

Any factual errors are mine, and I would appreciate having them pointed out. All images, unless otherwise indicated, are from the author's collection.

A customary Hawaiian language diacritical mark, the 'okina (glottal stop), is used in this book and signifies a clean break before or between vowels.

This book was supported in part by a grant from the Hawai'i Council for the Humanities.

INTRODUCTION

Hawai'i is the only state to have been a monarchy, republic, and territory. It has the only royal palace on U.S. soil, the most active volcano, and numerous plant and bird species found nowhere else in the world.

Hawai'i also enjoys a rich and largely unknown theatrical history.

British Royal Navy captain James Cook is credited with discovering the islands in 1774, which he named the Sandwich Islands in honor of his patron the Earl of Sandwich; however, a native indigenous population had inhabited Hawai'i since approximately 1100 AD.

Their location in the middle of the Pacific Ocean, 2,500 miles from the nearest land, made the islands a desirable, if not necessary, stopping point since the 18th century for explorers, traders, and merchant ships in their voyages between the United States, Asia, and the South Pacific. Hawai'i was also a mecca for early adventurers and authors such as Robert Louis Stevenson, Herman Melville, Jack London, and Mark Twain, who called Hawai'i "the loveliest fleet of islands that lies anchored in any ocean."

Protestant missionaries from Boston first arrived in 1820, and they frowned upon stage performances as immoral. Nonetheless, the growing population of American merchants and their families were hungry for familiar cultural entertainment—concerts, plays, musicals, and opera—and eventually began presenting them on an informal and impromptu basis around the capital city of Honolulu.

The first purpose-built theatre, the Thespian, appeared in Honolulu in September 1847. The Royal Hawaiian opened in June 1848, and the Varieties in September 1853. Nearly 30 years later, the Music Hall, later known as the Opera House, became the place to go, and it was there in 1897 that movies were first publicly shown in Hawai'i.

By the end of the first decade of the 20th century, there were a dozen nickelodeons in downtown Honolulu—places like the Art, Gem, Novelty, Royal, Savoy, and one named San Francisco. Larger and more modern theatres soon appeared, including the Bijou in 1910, and Ye Liberty in 1912 (which operated until 1984).

Honolulu gained its first and only major downtown theatres two months apart in 1922, the Hawai'i and the Princess. Although they were not as large or elaborate as the movie palaces built later in the decade throughout the mainland U.S., they were the biggest and fanciest Hawai'i had seen.

In 1928, the introduction of modern talking pictures in Honolulu created excitement that caused a sharp rise in movie attendance. This, in turn, led to the widespread remodeling of older theatres and the building of dozens of new neighborhood movie houses throughout the 1930s in Honolulu and on the neighbor islands.

At the time, the main industry in Hawai'i was agriculture, with more than three dozen sugar cane and pineapple plantations throughout the islands producing products for the U.S. market.

These plantations imported laborers from many different countries and housed them in plantation-built communities. As few of the workers owned cars, the plantations built theatres and other recreational facilities for them. These plantation theatres were typically plain, with walls and roof of corrugated sheet metal, a flat wooden or concrete floor, and simple benches for seating. Films were shown weekly for each ethnic group—Japanese, Chinese, Puerto Rican, and Filipino. The theatres also regularly featured live ethnic entertainment. With the eventual demise of the sugar and pineapple industries, the theatres were put to other uses, demolished, or just abandoned; many still exist in rural areas.

Outside the plantations, there were theatres that screened ethnic films exclusively, and second-run houses whose weekly schedule included something in a different language each night.

World War II brought hundreds of thousands of servicemen to the islands, and both military and civilian theatres alike did excellent business in spite of wartime curfews and other restrictions. But after the war, shifts in population and movie-going habits, along with the challenge of television in the 1950s, caused the demise of many neighborhood theatres.

The last few new, freestanding theatres were built in the 1960s, but then the twinning and multiplexing began, and soon theatres opened in shopping malls. Some old movie houses found new uses as churches or retail space, while others were simply closed and left to decay.

Demolition claimed dozens of theatres, some after a valiant struggle to save them, while others simply disappeared without notice or comment. Years later, many residents lamented over what had been lost and realized that more of an effort should have been made to preserve some for reuse.

Among the major losses, the saddest was the Waikiki, a 1936 tropical moderne jewel, once Hawai'i's most uniquely beautiful theatre, although greatly altered in later years. It was demolished in 2005 due to declining attendance and escalating property values. The 1938 Toyo was another great loss. Designed in a finely detailed Asian style, it was a beautiful, richly decorated theatre, inside and out, and had a great potential for reuse.

Those that were spared from the wrecking ball (or these days, the hydraulic crawler excavator) have been few, but significant:

Honolulu's 1922 Hawai'i was saved by a group of dedicated individuals, including this author, beginning in 1984. With the enthusiastic support of business and community leaders, the State of Hawai'i, and over $30 million invested in the structure's restoration and renovation, this neoclassical gem is now a successful performing arts center.

The 1925 Palace in Hilo, on the "Big Island" of Hawai'i, was also saved and reopened by community effort. It is currently undergoing a grassroots restoration while showcasing varied popular entertainment, including films, theatre, and musical performances.

The 'Iao (1928) in Wailuku, Maui, was purchased and restored by the County of Maui, and is used regularly as a community performing arts center.

Other theatres such as the People's in Honoka'a and Aloha in Kainaliu, both on the Island of Hawai'i, are well cared for by dedicated individuals and serve their communities with a wide range of entertainment.

Among the few remaining now-shuttered theatres that could again become a vibrant part of the community are the 1936 Queen in Honolulu; the Waimea in Waimea, Kaua'i; the Na'alehu in the town of the same name; and Kona in Kainaliu (the latter two on Hawai'i).

Well over 400 theatres have existed in Hawai'i in the nearly 125 years from 1847 to 1969. A great many eluded ever being photographed, but more than 80 of them are included in this book. Many others have equally interesting histories, which hopefully will be publicized one day.

The theatres in Hawai'i today are vastly different than in decades past. In terms of decor, they've come full circle, from plain, storefront nickelodeons of yesteryear, through exotic designs of the 1920s and 1930s, to the comfortably plain, draped, box-like techno-cocoons of present day. This book celebrates the way they were back then for those who may fondly remember them, as well as others who never knew them.

The author is very interested in any Hawaiian theatre memories, historical information, or photographs anyone is willing to share. He may be contacted at theatresofhawaii@mail.com.

One

EARLY YEARS IN THE
KINGDOM OF HAWAI'I

The first permanent, albeit short-lived, theatre, the Thespian, opened September 11, 1847, in a leased building. Seats in the pit were 50¢ and $1 in the boxes. There was also a royal box for King Kamehameha III. The theatre closed within a few months, but was reborn in 1848. Renamed the Royal Hawaiian, it was described as a "quaint, old-fashioned building in the midst of a beautiful garden," located in what was then a residential area. In 1852 and 1855, actor Edwin Booth, brother of Lincoln assassin (and actor) John Wilkes Booth, performed during his brief stopovers. After nearly 30 years, in 1879 the Royal Hawaiian closed and was demolished by 1881.

The city's next theatre, the Varieties, opened in September 1853. Described as a "big shell" of a place, it presented the first amateur opera in the islands in February 1854, Donizetti's *Daughter of the Regiment*. The program also noted that an "efficient police will be . . . in attendance," perhaps because of the many, sometimes rowdy, sailors in the port town. The Varieties burned down the following year.

When the Honolulu Music Hall opened in 1881, built by sugar and banking millionaire William G. Irwin at a cost of $40,000, it was praised as "an ornament and an honor to the City." It also had a royal box with a private entrance for King Kalakaua. The theatre went bankrupt within two years, but was reopened. During the 1889 Wilcox Rebellion, troops were stationed on its roof to protect 'Iolani Palace, directly across the street. The Music Hall burned to the ground in 1895, but was rebuilt by Irwin, with partners John and Adolph Spreckels. It reopened the following year as the Hawaiian Opera House.

It was at the Hawaiian Opera House that the first moving pictures were publicly shown in Hawai'i in February 1897, just two years after modern motion picture projection was perfected. Amazed audiences viewed seven brief scenes of Hawai'i, filmed in Edison's Veriscope by his cameramen during an island stopover. Copies of these films exist in the Library of Congress.

The Royal Hawaiian, Honolulu's second theatre, opened in 1848 at the corner of Hotel and Alakea Streets, then a residential area. Its owners operated the city's first theatre, the Thespian, in an adobe building at King and Maunakea Streets the year before. The Royal Hawaiian's inaugural season was cut short because so many local residents left for the California Gold Rush. The theatre closed in 1879 and was later demolished. (Courtesy Hawai'i State Archives.)

Musical News.

PUBLISHED BY SHERMAN, HYDE & CO., SAN FRANCISCO.

MUSIC HALL
HONOLULU, H. I.
THURSDAY EVEN'G, JAN. 13, 1881
OPENING NIGHT, AND
BENEFIT OF THE BUILDING FUND!
When will be presented in the presence of
HIS MAJESTY THE KING.
The great romantic play in a prologue and four acts, entitled
THE MARBLE HEART!
OR, THE SCULPTOR'S DREAM.

Characters in the Dream:

PHIDIAS (the Sculptor)	CHAS. B. WELLS
DIOGENES (the cynic philosopher)	HENRY N. WILSON
GORGIAS (a rich citizen of Athens)	W. C. CROSBIE
ALCIBIADES (the General)	J. M. FRANCOEUR
THEA (a slave)	MISS ELIZA LONG
ASPASIA	MISS MAY WILKES
LAIS (statues)	MISS ELLA ALLEN
PHRYNE	MISS EMMA FLEMING

Characters in the Play:

RAPHAEL DUCHALET (a sculptor)	CHAS. B. WELLS
FERDINAND VOLAGE (an editor)	HENRY N. WILSON
MONS. VEAUDORE (a rich Parisian)	W. C. CROSBIE
VIS. CHATEAUMARGAUX (with song)	J. M. FRANCOEUR
FRED DeCOURCY (a butterfly)	H. F. MORTON
JOHN (a footman)	C. S. GREGORY
M'LLE. MARCO (The Marble Heart)	MISS MAY WILKES
M'LLE. CLEMENTINE (her friend)	MISS ELLA ALLEN
M'LLE. MARRIETTE (another)	MRS. MABLE CLOSSON
FEDORA	MISS EMMA FLEMING
MARIE (a poor orphan)	MISS ELIZA LONG
MADAME DUCHALET (Raphael's mother)	MISS ELLA ALLEN

Synopsis of Scenery and Incidents.

Prologue—The Dream. *Scene, Studio of Phidias at Athens.* Time, 360, B. C.

The rich Gorgias; the fortunate Alcibiades; the poor Sculptor; Diogenes and his lantern; the statues; which do they choose—love or money? "Ah! Marble Hearts! Marble Hearts!!" Tableau—Curtain.

ACT 1st.—Time, the present; Scene, the Forest of Fontainbleau. Characters of the Dream in real life: A picnic; song, "Chink of Gold;" Diogenes, an editor in real life; The poor orphan; the dreamer arrives; Raphael sees "the statues of his dream;" Fascination; the presentiment of evil.

ACT 2nd.—Raphael's studio; his infatuation for Marco; a mother's love; a friend's advice; a storm and what it brings; the orphan's story; modesty and virtue as against an evil fascination; which will win? "Dead to all but Marco's love."

ACT 3rd.—"The Marble Heart" at home; a rich marriage the aim of her life; Raphael's dream fulfilled; Marco renounces his love; his despair; a friend's interference; its result; "for you I renounce all;" Marco's story; "Gold! Gold! Gold!" Breaking hearts; "Adieu, Marco, forever."

ACT 4th.—Home again; the prodigal's return; atonement for the past; the funeral wreath; "I am a murderer;" Marie's love; insanity; despair; death; "Marble Hearts! Marble Hearts! woe to the man who loves you; thou hast ever been, and ever will be, ministers of ruin, misery and death!" Tableau—The End.

☞ Special attention is called to the Scenery by W. T. Porter, of the first and third acts. The furniture used in the third act was manufactured by C. E. Williams, Fort St.

Saturday Night, "OUR BOYS."

The beauty of a bass drum is only skin deep.

Adelina Patti receives about $7.00 a minute while singing in opera.

Sherman, Hyde & Co., have the largest Music House in San Francisco.

The Ark must have been a poker deck by the number of pairs she held.

Saint-Sæns having recovered from his indisposition, has returned to Paris.

We will send full and complete catalogues of all kinds of musical merchandise upon application.

Chicago has a lawyer named Music. "Ah, yes! "Music hath charms to sue the savage.

Belgium has 2,600 harmonic societies, 3,000 choral societies, and 31 royal conservatories of music.

A McTammany Organette will give more real enjoyment in a household, than can be secured for the price if invested in anything else.

Miss Griswold, a niece of Bret Harte, has just gained a prize for singing at the Paris Conservatoire.

The Sherman, Hyde & Co., Uprights are warranted to stand the most variable climates. They are first-class in every respect, and sold at the low price of $350.

Julia Wilson, (Little Tot), of Joshua Whitcomb's troupe, has lately inherited twelve thousand dollars from her grandfather, the late Wm. Wilson, of Westchester County, N. Y.

$350 purchases one of our new Sherman, Hyde & Co., Upright Pianos. They are "as good as the best," and no one need ask for a better.

From all parts of the coast we have received expressions of gratitude from parties who have received our popular $4 German accordeons with two sets of reeds—one stop. In nearly every instance great surprise has been manifested that we can send so good an Instrument for so small a sum.

This is a newsletter advertising the Music Hall's opening night program on January 13, 1881, attended by King Kalakaua. This is the same play Abraham Lincoln saw John Wilkes Booth perform in November 9, 1863, while sitting in the presidential box at Ford's Theatre in Washington, D.C. Sherman, Hyde, and Company, a San Francisco firm, sold musical instruments in Hawai'i and is still in business today as Sherman Clay.

11

This photograph shows the Music Hall, right. It was taken from the second floor of the 'Iolani Palace, across the street. The Hawaiian flag flies near Ali'iolani Hale, which was completed in 1874 and originally designed as the royal palace. It was modified to house the Hawaiian government, legislature, and supreme court. It is still the home of the state supreme court today. (Courtesy Mission Houses Museum Library.)

Designed by C. J. Wall, one of the architects of 'Iolani Palace, the brick Music Hall seated around 800. A description noted, "Gas has been introduced at great expense, the auditorium being lighted from the dome by a sunburner of 40 jets. This most important factor will be utilized in producing moonlight, sunsets and storm effects upon the stage." It did not mention the danger of fire. (Courtesy Hawai'i State Archives.)

The 50-member cast of Gilbert and Sullivan's *The Mikado* is shown in costume and onstage at the Music Hall in April 1890. The six musicians in the orchestra appear to be waiting for their next cue. Note the gas lighting fixtures above the arched boxes on each side of the stage. (Courtesy Hawai'i State Archives.)

Spectators watch as fire destroys the Music Hall on the morning of February 12, 1895. This photograph was taken from the tower of Ali'iolani Hale. The domed structure in the upper right corner is the pavilion built for the coronation of King Kalakaua and Queen Kapi'olani in 1883. It was moved and later used as a bandstand on the grounds of 'Iolani Palace. (Courtesy Hawai'i State Archives.)

The new Opera House, pictured here in March 1908, was designed by architects C. B. Ripley and C. W. Dickey. It opened November 8, 1896, with *Il Trovatore*, codirected by Henri Berger. Three months later on February 5, 1897, the first movies publicly presented in Hawai'i were shown. (Courtesy Hawai'i State Archives.)

The ample stage of the Opera House measured 60 feet wide and 42 feet deep and boasted "485 incandescent lamps in all, of the Hawaiian Electric Company." The proscenium arch was described as "bordered by 21 gilded ornamental panels of a Renaissance design, each with a lamp," while the four proscenium boxes were of "quasi Hindoo-Moorish type, the front balustrading, however, being an acanthus leaf motif." (Courtesy Punahou School Archives)

With an advertised "capacity of 1,000, with seating for 600," this appears to be an almost-full house at the Opera House, including some standees in the back. With the men in suits and ladies in long-sleeved long dresses, it could not have been very comfortable on a hot day, even with the large ventilating fan on and the trade winds blowing through the open windows. (Courtesy Mission Houses Museum Library.)

All was not highbrow entertainment at the Opera House, as shown by this Honolulu Elk's Lodge *Grand Operatic and Minstrel Show* program in 1909. Among the 22 musical numbers were songs such as "She Borrowed My Only Husband and Forgot to Bring Him Back." It also included the Honolulu Concert Orchestra performing "The Teddy Bear's Picnic," and motion pictures of local scenes by Honolulu photographer R. K. Bonine.

Charles Desky opened the Orpheum on Fort Street above Beretania Street on December 11, 1898. Entrepreneur-turned-showman Joel C. Cohen took over the following year and presented vaudeville and traveling shows. In 1901, Jesse Lasky played cornet in the orchestra for $25 a week; he later became a pioneer film producer and cofounder of what is now Paramount Pictures. The Orpheum regularly showed movies beginning in 1906. It burned down on April 28, 1910.

Two

The New Territory of Hawai'i

Once moving pictures were first shown, the fad caught on quickly and numerous nickelodeons appeared in Honolulu. The earliest were little more than small converted storefronts.

The first major new purpose-built theatre was the Orpheum, which opened in 1898 and, apart from the Opera House, was the largest theatre in Honolulu, seating 945. The following year, it was taken over by Joel C. Cohen, a former fur-trader and soldier-of-fortune turned showman. In 1906, the Orpheum was the first to show movies on a regular basis. It did not last long, however; the theatre was destroyed by fire in 1910. Undaunted, Cohen took over another downtown theatre, the Bonine, and renamed it the New Orpheum.

By 1909, films were being shown regularly at the Opera House, which featured the first talking picture that year. An advertisement boasted, "First appearance in Honolulu of the Cameraphone, the machine that talks, sings, and acts." Eight other theatres advertised in the newspaper, including several open-air venues. Within a year, the number had increased to 14 theatres, plus two Chinese theatres.

In 1911, many of the independent theatre operators joined forces and formed the Honolulu Amusement Company, with Joel Cohen as president and J. Alfred Magoon as vice president.

In late 1912, they took over Ye Liberty, which opened February 22, 1912. Built of brick with steel roof trusses, it seated 1,600 and advertised itself as "Honolulu's safest theatre." The Liberty went through many changes over the years. It was completely gutted and modernized in 1929, then remodeled again in the late 1930s. A second-run movie house for most of its life, it enjoyed a long 72-year run, closing in 1984 and was demolished in 1990 to make way for a parking lot.

In 1913, Cohen and John Henry Magoon, J. Alfred's son, bought out their partners and formed Consolidated Amusement Company, which became the largest circuit of the islands, eventually operating more than three dozen theatres at its peak. The company continues today as Hawai'i's oldest and largest theatre operator, nearing its centennial.

The first theatre for Japanese drama was the Asahi located at the corner of Beretania and Maunakea Streets. It opened in 1899, but was destroyed by the Chinatown fire of 1900. The second Asahi, seen here, opened at 1162 Maunakea Street near Pauahi Street in 1908. Built of wood, it had a large stage, a balcony, several dressing rooms, and stores on the street. It was demolished by 1928. (Courtesy Bishop Museum.)

Honolulu had numerous open-air moving picture theatres in the early years of the 20th century, thanks to the tropical climate. In the photograph above, the Park Theatre at Fort Street and Chaplain Lane hosts a full house for an unknown film. It advertised itself as "not an ill-smelling closed auditorium," and operated from 1909 to 1911. The Catholic cathedral and convent, both extant, can be seen above the fence. (Courtesy Hawai'i State Archives.)

The new Empire, designed by Honolulu architect H. L. Kerr, opened at Hotel and Bethel Streets on May 15, 1909, and was run by Frank Richardson and R. N. Overend. By 1913, it had become part of Consolidated Amusement Company and operated until 1933, when it was demolished. The present structure at that location is known as the Empire Building. (L. E. Edgeworth photograph. Courtesy Bishop Museum.)

This March 1913 photograph advertises several silent films and shorts. With 930 seats, the Empire was called "the most artistic playhouse in town, with perfect acoustics," while the stage was said to be the "largest in the city." It also had a photoplayer, a type of organ with orchestral and percussion instruments and various sound effects. (L. E. Edgeworth photograph. Courtesy Bishop Museum.)

Joel Cohen's Orpheum burned down in April 1910. By June, he had leased the Bonine Theatre on Hotel Street as the new Orpheum. In the interim, he likely operated this temporary open-air theatre on Bishop Street, Cohen's Red Light Opera House, possibly during a local fair. The red light probably refers, with a little irony, to red lights used by the fire department. (Courtesy Hawaiian Historical Society.)

Two unidentified men stand in front of the Honolulu Theatre on Hotel Street. Like most early nickelodeons, it was a converted storefront with a capacity of 100 to 200 patrons. (Courtesy Bishop Museum.)

The Bijou was located between Pauahi and Hotel Streets, fronting what later became Bethel Street, and opened December 4, 1910. This photograph was taken February 12, 1911, at the Pauahi entrance. The young men are identified as "Mashadow, Joe, ? at wheel, Lino, Klemmy, Frank." Perhaps they were actors or musicians (note the case on the fender), attending the show, or just driving around. At any rate, the moment was captured in time.

The Bijou's main entrance was at the end of a short alley off Hotel Street known as Bijou Lane. The James Post Company advertised here was one of many traveling stock companies. The theatre was demolished in 1921 and replaced by the present Hawai'i Theatre, but Bijou Lane survived until 1989 when the City created the Chinatown Gateway Park. (L .E. Edgeworth photograph. Courtesy Bishop Museum.)

Above is the interior of the Bijou in March 1913. Built by J. Alfred Magoon and H. Rosenberg, it had 1,600 seats, an eight-piece orchestra and, as evidenced, no decor. Primitive talking pictures, four short films in Edison's Kinetophone process, using recorded celluloid cylinders connected to the projector by a long pulley mechanism, were shown here August 5, 1915. Not surprisingly, the contraption never worked very well. (L. E. Edgeworth photograph. Courtesy Bishop Museum.)

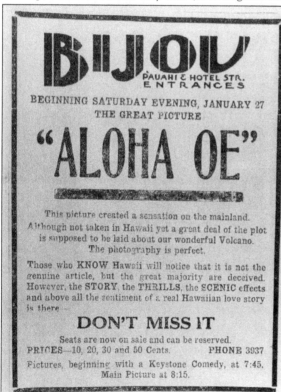

Aloha Oe opened at the Bijou on January 27, 1917. One of the early films with Hawaiian themes, it was a Hollywood-produced stereotype, with hula maidens and erupting volcanoes. As the advertisement said, "It is not the genuine article, but the great majority are deceived." The film featured Frank Borzage, later an esteemed director, and Enid Markey, who enjoyed a six-decade-long acting career.

Whatever the show was at Bailey and Lawson's Art Theatre on Hotel Street around 1908, the men in the projection booth were ready as patrons crowded the aisles for it. Apart from the ladies' large hats, there was nothing fancy in this theatre, as open knob and tube wiring ran along the walls, just below the corrugated tin roof. Even with the open windows, the small wall fans could not have helped much. It closed in 1910 after only three years of operation. (L. E. Edgeworth photograph. Courtesy Bishop Museum.)

The Savoy opened January 5, 1910, on Hotel Street near Bethel and was managed by Jack Scully and Eugene Love. The arched open vestibule on the sidewalk was typical of many nickelodeons. There was no inner lobby, so patrons entered directly into the auditorium that was, according to the papers, "half open-air." This image is from 1913, when the Savoy was renamed the Hawaiʻi. It closed by 1921, before the present Hawaiʻi Theatre opened.

When it opened on February 22, 1912, the Liberty was billed as "Hawai'i's first fireproof theatre." In 1929, it was extensively remodeled with a modernized facade and a new interior, offering a large lobby and expanded stage. Acquired by Consolidated Amusement in 1934, it showed mostly second and third-run movies. In April 1965, it was leased, renamed Nikkatsu, and showed Japanese films for several years. After 72 years, the Liberty closed on July 4, 1984, and was demolished in 1990, becoming a parking lot. (L. E. Edgeworth photograph. Courtesy Bishop Museum.)

Well-dressed patrons attend a show at the Liberty in 1918, six years after it opened as Ye Liberty. By this time, after the "Ye" was dropped, the theatre had a new sign and large poster cases on the exterior promoting Paramount pictures. (L. E. Edgeworth photograph. Courtesy Bishop Museum.)

Above is a rare photograph of the Liberty's original interior taken on April 2, 1918, as a full house waits for the show to begin. The iron shutters are wide open to the outside, providing natural (and the only) ventilation. On the walls are murals of Hawaiian scenes painted by famed artist Lionel Walden, which still exist in private hands. Note the projectionist standing on the walkway to the left of the booth. (L. E. Edgeworth photograph. Courtesy Bishop Museum.)

The Liberty also hosted concerts, including one by locally born operatic tenor Tandy MacKenzie, and various events, such as this meeting of a Korean independence group around 1916. In the orchestra pit is the new Wurlitzer style YK photoplayer. It was a small pipe organ with many sound effects, played live or with music rolls, and used to accompany the silent films. (Courtesy Mrs. Yun Hee Chun Given.)

This is a Liberty Theatre program with its tasteful, yet somewhat risque cover for the week of May 10, 1919. It described the week's films and the stars, along with local advertisements, including Hawaiian Electric, which urged readers to "use electric service in your home;" Clarence Crabbe, seeking the Republican nomination for mayor (in English and Hawaiian); and "Madame Cleo, the noted Palmist," who offered a "special this month—$1 for both palms."

The Liberty auditorium walls featured these Moorish double-arched false windows with corbeled brackets, also known as a bifora. Installed during the 1929 remodeling, each had a different hand-painted scene mounted in it, which were softly illuminated during the show. Acoustical tiles stenciled with a decorative pattern lined the walls.

A lone sailor walks down Kamanuwai Lane towards the Beretania Theatre during World War II. The narrow lane, mauka of Beretania Street near Maunakea Street, was known as Tin Can Alley for its corrugated metal buildings. The 400-seat theatre dates from 1914. Purchased by William Ferreira in 1944, it showed mostly adult films. Renamed Beretania Follies in 1947, it began a 20-year run as Honolulu's first burlesque house, with *Cover Girl Scandals*. (Herbert Bauer photograph. Courtesy Bishop Museum.)

This advertising card with a map on the back was probably passed out to servicemen on nearby Hotel Street during World War II. Honolulu police tried to shut the theatre down, citing its shows as obscene. The judge, after seeing a performance, dismissed the charge, saying that it was "nothing more than you'd see on Waikiki Beach." The theatre, along with the entire area, was demolished as part of urban renewal in the late 1960s.

This Chinese theatre was built in 1920 on the site of an earlier 1903 Chinese theatre. It then became the Honolulu-za (Honolulu Theatre), showing Japanese films. Acquired by Consolidated in 1934, it was remodeled in 1939, and screened Hollywood second-run films during WWII, when Japanese movies were prohibited. The theatre and surrounding Japanese business district, demolished in the late 1960s for urban renewal, is now part of an expanded A'ala Park.

In this 1920s photograph, two little boys pose for the camera in front of the Honolulu-za. The sidewalk is lined with colorful banners promoting the Japanese movies, and two men are considering the latest attraction.

28

A well-dressed crowd waits to get into the Honolulu-za for a Japanese film, probably in the late 1930s or 1940s, while a policeman keeps order. Long before the age of television and videotape, this was the only way one could see such films. (Courtesy Hawai'i State Archives.)

Drivers with their taxis line up outside the first Pawa'a Theatre around 1918. Located on King Street, two blocks town side of Punahou Street, it was an open-air theatre with benches surrounded by high, corrugated metal walls. Patrons brought umbrellas in case of showers. Opened in 1916, it featured Japanese and later, Hollywood films. It closed by the time the newer Pawa'a Theatre opened in 1929. (U. Teragawatchi photograph. Courtesy Bishop Museum.)

The small Akebono Theatre in Pahoa on the Big Island opened December 7, 1917, and has the distinction of being the oldest extant theatre in the state. Of plain and simple design, it has a flat floor inside. Mounted in the attic is a small wooden plaque inscribed with Japanese characters for good luck and good fortune. (Courtesy State Historic Preservation Office.)

The Tip Top Theatre in Lihu'e, Kaua'i, which dates back to 1916, was among the first movie houses on the "Garden Island." Part of a large movie poster, probably promoting 1919's *The Drifter*, can be seen on the left of this 1920 photograph. The theatre closed in 1932, but a Tip Top building exists nearby today.

On the "Valley Island" of Maui, the Kahului Theatre, with its neoclassical design, opened May 17, 1918, at Main Street (later Ka'ahumanu Avenue) and Pu'unene Avenue, replacing an earlier theatre, the Kahului Lyceum, on the same site.

In the 1930s, the Kahului Theatre was remodeled and the facade sported a new streamlined moderne look with decorative vertical grilles. Several servicemen loiter on the sidewalk in this 1944 photograph. The posters advertise *Flesh and Fantasy* and *Woman of the Town*. A favorite of local residents during its 45 years of operation, the theatre was demolished around 1963 to make way for the expansion of a shopping center.

Located near the large Hawaiian Commercial and Sugar Company mill, the Pu'unene Theatre on Maui served the plantation community and its many workers camps for decades following the time this photograph was taken around 1923. The theatre advertises Eddie Polo's *The Secret Four*. The mill, built in 1901, is still in operation, but the theatre stopped showing movies in the mid-1960s, and was then demolished. (Courtesy Alexander and Baldwin Sugar Museum.)

Lahaina's 1913 Pioneer Theatre, with signs on the wall in Japanese, was located directly behind the Pioneer Inn, the two-story building next to the horse and cart. The historic hotel, built in 1901 by George Freeland, is still in operation. The theatre is long gone, replaced in 1965 by a wing of hotel rooms and shops. (Ray Jerome Baker photograph. Courtesy Bishop Museum.)

Three

Downtown Palaces and More Playhouses

Downtown was the business and social center of Honolulu, where most theatres stood and newer, larger ones would be constructed.

The largest ever built, the Hawai'i and the Princess, were two blocks away from each other and opened two months apart in 1922. They were the closest the islands ever had to later mainland-style movie palaces, though not as big or elegant as their counterparts.

In 1918, local leaders, including Hawai'i's Prince Jonah Kuhio and Prince David Kawananakoa, began planning the People's Theatre, envisioned as being equal to any theatre of its kind in the United States. Honolulu architects Clinton B. Ripley, Louis Davis, and Ralph Fishbourne's Beaux Arts design featured a large stage and stadium-style seating for 1,650. When the building was half finished, the company ran out of money. Acquired by San Francisco theatre operator Louis Greenfield, it was renamed the New Princess, completed, and opened November 8, 1922. The Princess was always considered the people's favorite, as it was known for popular stage entertainment. Acquired in 1925 by Consolidated Amusement, it was extensively remodeled in 1939. Following the World War II boom years, it became the first home of Cinerama in 1958 before being demolished in 1969, the victim of urban renewal.

In 1920, Consolidated Amusement started plans for its deluxe theatre, the Bijou, which they conceived as early as 1912. Renamed the Hawai'i, it was designed by local architects Walter Emory and Marshall Webb in a neoclassical style. The $260,000 building opened September 6, 1922, and was the company's flagship until the Waikiki Theatre opened in 1936.

After the 1930s and 1940s boom years, the Hawai'i held on in the 1950s, but then began to decline. It became a second, then third-run house, degenerating into showing soft-core adult films before closing in 1984. A dedicated group, including this author, rallied to save the theatre, and eventually it was renovated before reopening as a modern performing arts center.

Large urban theatres, such as the Palace in Hilo and the 'Iao in Wailuku, Maui, also opened on the neighbor islands. Both enjoy life today as restored performing arts centers.

Ground is broken in June 1921 for the new Hawai'i Theatre downtown, originally planned as the new Bijou. Standing on the old Bijou's site are Joel Cohen (with straw hat and cigar), president of Consolidated Amusement Company, formed in 1913, and treasurer John Henry Magoon (smiling). Looking on is probably one of the architects, Walter Emory or Marshall Webb, along with John Mason Young, president of the builders, Pacific Engineering Company. A successful businessman, Cohen was also a legislator in 1909 and ran for mayor twice.

Harold Lloyd's comedy *Dr. Jack* was on the screen for a week starting May 27, 1923, when this picture was taken. Movies had been shown at the Hawai'i since the day after it opened. The small readerboard on the corner of the building was replaced by a larger one. The marquee over the entrance also went through a number of changes over the years. (Courtesy Terry Helgesen Collection, Theatre Historical Society of America.)

34

This large 52-page commemorative program was published soon after the theatre's gala opening on September 6, 1922, which was attended by Governor Wallace Rider Farrington. Tickets were a pricey $2 to $4. The program's revealing, yet classically tasteful cover probably caused some comment in 1920s Honolulu. Filled with photographs (some of which are included in this book), it described in great detail and florid language the theatre's genesis, as well as its many notable features, among them a unique double-cantilever supporting the balcony.

The outer lobby of the Hawaiʻi was originally open to the sidewalk, with the box office located on the left. Through the doors, one of the marble statues, part of the theatre's extensive art collection, can be seen. The lobby is now enclosed for security and comfort, the ticket window has been put back, and the marble statues donated back to the theatre by Consolidated Amusement. (Courtesy Terry Helgesen Collection, Theatre Historical Society of America.)

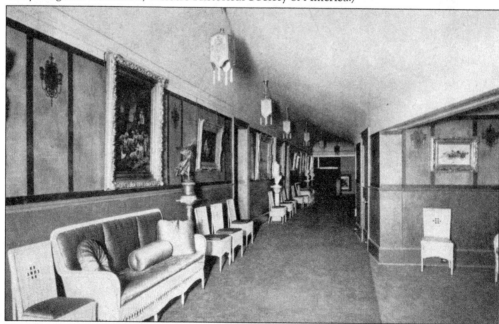

The new Hawaiʻi cost an estimated $500,000, and among its furnishings was an extensive art collection, displayed in the mezzanine gallery seen here and in the offices. A 1925 inventory listed more than two dozen works by prominent artists, including a painting of Indians by Frederic Remington, which hangs on the wall at right. The whereabouts of these works today is unknown. (Courtesy Terry Helgesen Collection, Theatre Historical Society of America.)

Above is a view from the stage toward the wide, yet shallow auditorium. In the lobby, barely visible between the curtains, are three marble statues. The chair cushions and backs were covered in real grasscloth, which was said to provide cool comfort but probably did not hold up well. On either side of the projection booth were private boxes, each with five seats.

When this photograph of the balcony was taken in August 1922, a month before the theatre's opening, workmen were still putting the finishing touches on the new 1,760-seat Hawai'i. The sidewall windows and doors were all open to the trade winds. The loge boxes, separated by velour curtains, contained wicker chairs with cushions featuring a stylized "H" design. This design has been replicated in the present seats.

Daylight streams through the windows in this September 1922 view of the right side of the auditorium. The draped organ chamber grille rises above the box seats. The 4-manual 15-rank Robert Morton pipe organ cost $42,500. The sparkle of the newly gilded decor is evident. The edge of the orchestra pit can also be seen; the Hawai'i had a full-time 8-piece orchestra, dismissed in 1929 after sound films began. (Courtesy Terry Helgesen Collection, Theatre Historical Society of America.)

This photograph from 1968 displays the painting by famed artist Lionel Walden on the sounding board above the proscenium. Titled *The Procession of the Drama*, it was damaged in the late 1970s when the roof leaked and the plaster under the painting fell to the floor, taking the left half of the work with it. The mess was promptly thrown out by the custodian. Fortunately, it was replicated from pictures by artists with Conrad Schmitt Studios.

The star's dressing room above may not seem luxurious by today's standards, but it was for a theatre in 1922. There was even a sunken Roman tub in the next room. Remarkably, the table, chair, and chandelier survived backstage at the theatre until the mid-1980s. (Courtesy Terry Helgesen Collection, Theatre Historical Society of America.)

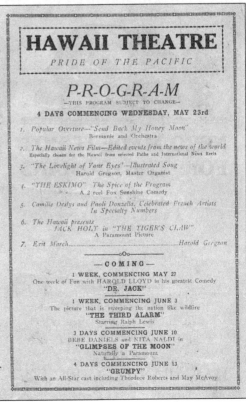

HAWAII THEATRE
PRIDE OF THE PACIFIC

P-R-O-G-R-A-M
—THIS PROGRAM SUBJECT TO CHANGE—

4 DAYS COMMENCING WEDNESDAY, MAY 23rd

1. *Popular Overture—"Send Back My Honey Moon"*
  Bermanie and Orchestra

2. *The Hawaii News Film—Edited events from the news of the world*
  Especially chosen for the Hawaii from selected Pathe and International News Reels

3. *"The Lovelight of Your Eyes"—Illustrated Song*
  Harold Gregson, Master Organist

4. *"THE ESKIMO" The Spice of the Program*
  A 2 reel Fox Sunshine Comedy

5. *Camille Deslys and Paoli Donzella, Celebrated French Artists*
  In Specialty Numbers

6. *The Hawaii presents*
  JACK HOLT in "THE TIGER'S CLAW"
  A Paramount Picture

7. *Exit March*..........................Harold Gregson

———oOo———

——— COMING ———

1 WEEK, COMMENCING MAY 27
One week of Fun with HAROLD LLOYD in his greatest Comedy
"DR. JACK"

1 WEEK, COMMENCING JUNE 3
The picture that is sweeping the nation like wildfire
"THE THIRD ALARM"
Starring Ralph Lewis

3 DAYS COMMENCING JUNE 10
BEBE DANIELS and NITA NALDI in
"GLIMPSES OF THE MOON"
Naturally a Paramount

4 DAYS COMMENCING JUNE 13
"GRUMPY"
With an All-Star cast including Theodore Roberts and May McAvoy

Patrons certainly got their money's worth when they attended the Hawai'i in the early 1920s. The program, which began May 23, 1923, included an overture by the Hawai'i Theatre orchestra, a newsreel, the organist's rendition of an illustrated song, a two-reel comedy, and a live act before the picture. After the film, the organist played an exit march. What more could you ask for?

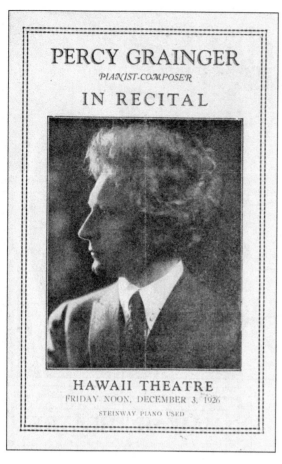

PERCY GRAINGER

PIANIST-COMPOSER

IN RECITAL

HAWAII THEATRE
FRIDAY NOON, DECEMBER 3, 1926
STEINWAY PIANO USED

Famed composer and pianist Percy Grainger appeared in a noontime concert at the Hawai'i on December 3, 1926. His performance had been rescheduled when the steamer he was traveling on was delayed on its way to Honolulu.

Both the Hawai'i and the Princess featured vaudeville along with movies throughout the 1920s. Among the many performers was Long Tack Sam, a juggler and magician, who appeared with his Great China Troupe, which included his two daughters. Although Hawai'i's population was heavily Asian, he was not a local performer, but rather a seasoned national touring vaudevillian. For many years, his painted, signed caricature was on the wall of the fly gallery backstage at the Hawai'i.

Publicity for the 1928 Gary Cooper–Colleen Moore film *Lilac Time*, about American and British pilots in World War I, included a makeshift lighted airplane atop the marquee. The box office of the six-year-old theatre had already been moved to face the sidewalk. (Y. Char photograph. Courtesy Bishop Museum.)

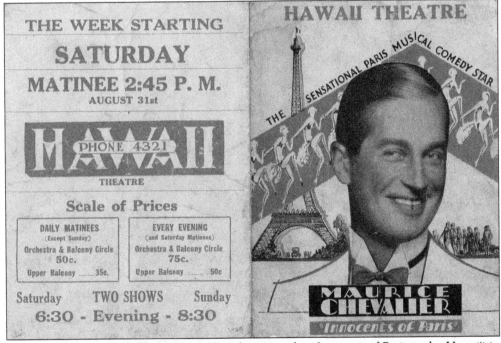

The inimitable Frenchman Maurice Chevalier starred in *Innocents of Paris* at the Hawai'i in August 1929, a month after sound films began regularly being shown there. This was Chevalier's first American film and first talkie, and of course, he sang numbers such as "Louise," among other tunes. It was also the first musical produced by Paramount Pictures. (Courtesy Desoto Brown.)

The famous fictional Hawaiian detective Charlie Chan (based upon a real Honolulu Police detective) was on screen at the Hawai'i on December 11, 1931. Scenes were filmed on location at the Royal Hawaiian Hotel, then just five years old, and elsewhere on O'ahu. Also in the cast in a supporting role was Bela Lugosi, who starred in *Dracula* that same year.

This view from around 1936 shows the second incarnation of the marquee with decorative panels added, as well as a new vertical sign. The huge wrap-around neon marquee was still a couple years in the future. Apart from that, nothing much has changed, other than the surrounding buildings and the direction of traffic.

The Hawai'i's unadorned lobby spaces received a locally crafted tropical moderne makeover around 1936. Above the tubular steel table, the starburst-framed mirror and a similar ceiling light were finished in Dutch metal leaf, as was the tall chevron-design wall panel. The pilaster featured an abstract Hawaiian design, flanked by a crosshatched plastered wall. The exotic maiden's faces, complete with hand-painted peacock feather surrounds, were lighting sconces. These elements were removed during 1990s renovations.

This ornate door, from the mezzanine to Consolidated Amusement's president's office, was added in the remodeling around 1936. It was a mélange of moderne elements, gilded in Dutch metal or painted in silver and pale turquoise—a potted cactus (carved on a masonite panel), surrounded by vines in plaster relief, surmounted with a fanciful deco pediment with what looked like the face of William Shakespeare. This deco delight was removed in the 1990s renovation.

Another creation of the 1936 makeover was this intricate plaster grille on the mezzanine stairs to the balcony. Painted in sliver and pale turquoise, it was both decorative and covered an original window. The plaster piece on the ceiling above, in the form of woven lauhala, hibiscus, and other tropical flowers, hid the spotlight for the panel. The bare bulb was part of an emergency lighting system installed later.

Crowds of patrons, including many sailors, line up under the neon marquee for the world premiere of *A Girl, a Guy, and a Gob* at the Hawai'i on March 4, 1941. Note the Shore Patrol officer at left, there to keep the sailors in line. Besides starring Lucille Ball, the film was the first of two movies famed comedian Harold Lloyd produced for RKO.

In 1946, a year after the war ended, sailors wait to get in to see a B-Western, Universal's *The Daltons Ride Again*. The Hawai'i's elaborate marquee may well have been more entertaining than the movie. (Ray Jerome Baker photograph. Courtesy Bishop Museum.)

This unique view of the Hawai'i was taken in 1986, two years after the effort to save the theatre began. It was the 50th anniversary of the publication of *Gone with the Wind*, and the film was restored for the occasion. The screening was a benefit for the theatre restoration, and more than 600 attended, many in period costume. The prize for best costume was a pair of airline tickets to Atlanta. (Courtesy *Honolulu Star-Advertiser*.)

The grand neon marquee from around 1938 blazed for more than 50 years until it fell into disrepair and was removed during renovation of the theatre in the early 1990s. Subsequently a decision was made to replace it and Young Electric Sign Company of Las Vegas created an amazingly accurate $1 million replication, complete with extensive neon and new electronic display panels. (Courtesy Young Electric Sign Company.)

The Princess Theatre, on Fort Street above Beretania Street, began construction as the People's Theatre in 1920, a year before the Hawai'i. It became a race to see which would open first. Unforeseen financial problems delayed completion of the Princess, which finally opened two months after the Hawai'i, on November 8, 1922, with *Sherlock Holmes*. Opening night tickets were a bargain at 25¢ to 75¢. (Courtesy Terry Helgesen Collection, Theatre Historical Society of America.)

Above is the ornate plant-filled lobby of the Princess when it opened in 1922. Stadium-style seating allowed for a very large lobby space below; the ramps on either side led to the upper seating. The gala opening was attended by Governor Wallace Rider Farrington, probably relaxing after the day's election of a new delegate to Congress, a seat made vacant by the death of Prince Kuhio in January. (Courtesy Desoto Brown.)

The interior of the 1,650-seat Princess, designed by architects Clinton B. Ripley, Louis Davis, and Ralph Fishbourne, proves that stadium-style seating is nothing new. A stunning element was the elaborately coffered ceiling. Seats in the loge and stepped side boxes had linen slipcovers, while those in the dress circle were upholstered in real grass cloth.

Seen here is the enormous proscenium in 1922. Although the Princess seated 110 fewer than the Hawai'i, the interior space was much larger and longer. With seats extending up to the back wall, when one sat in the last row, they were far from the stage. In the theatre's conversion to Cinerama in 1958, the booths for the three projectors were placed at the two side loge boxes and halfway up the center section.

In this photograph, half of the Robert Morton pipe organ for the Princess sits at the factory. After being built, each organ was completely assembled and tested, then taken apart, packed in crates, and shipped to the theatre, where it was carefully installed. Just prior to the 1969 Princess demolition, the organ was saved and moved two blocks to the Hawai'i Theatre, where it was eventually reinstalled and can still be enjoyed today.

To the right is an autographed program of world-famous violinist Yehudi Menuhin at the Princess in 1935, just short of his 19th birthday. A child prodigy, his first concert appearance was at age 7. Lyric tenor Tito Schipa and violinists Jascha Heifetz and Fritz Kreisler also played the Princess, the 1930s home of Honolulu Symphony concerts, under conductor Fritz Hart. The concerts began promptly at 9:00 p.m., after the last movie.

PRINCESS THEATER
YEHUDI MENUHIN

TWILIGHT CONCERT
Friday, April 5th, 1935

A sell-out crowd jams the sidewalk in each direction on February 12, 1938, to see Cary Grant and Irene Dunne's latest hit film *The Awful Truth*, followed by the popular Saturday evening Princess Pot Luck Show.

Always sold-out favorites at the Princess were the weekly Pot Luck Shows featuring island entertainers. *Hawaiian Halloween* was onstage October 28, 1939, with Kanekapolei and her World's Fair-est Hula Girls, who had just returned from a mainland tour. Premiering in September 1936, the shows started at 10:00 p.m. after the last film. The Pot Luck Shows—and peacetime—ended with *Tantalizing Tootsies*, a musical comedy revue, on Saturday, December 6, 1941.

A packed house for *Hawaiian Halloween* Pot Luck Show, with nearly every one of the 1,650 seats occupied. Among the well-known entertainers who appeared at these shows were Clara Inter (as Hilo Hattie), Lena Machado, John K. Almeida, Johnny Noble, and young Emma Veary. Among the many local groups featured were Joe Ikeole's Waialae Serenaders, Amy Kalima and her Hawaiians, and Henry Leoiki's Melody Islanders.

The Princess, newly remodeled by architect Vladimir Ossipoff, hosted the world premiere of the musical *Hawaiian Nights* on September 1, 1939, at 10:00 p.m. The crowds were perhaps unaware that Hitler had just invaded Poland, precipitating World War II. They line up, at left, for the 40¢ seats, with the 25¢ line on the right. In spite of being well attended, the movie was considered typical "Hollywood Hawaiian hokum." (Courtesy Terry Helgesen Collection, Theatre Historical Society of America.)

In 1958, the Princess became the 13th location in the country to be equipped for the new panoramic film sensation, Cinerama, which featured three projectors and a deeply curved wide screen. In this photograph, crowds gather for the premiere of the first film, *This Is Cinerama*, on July 22, 1958. The vertical neon sign alternately spelled "P-R-I-N-C-E-S-S" and "C-I-N-E-R-A-M-A."

Among the many notables attending the Princess/Cinerama premiere was longtime Honolulu sheriff (and Olympic champion swimmer and surfing legend) Duke Kahanamoku, seen here with his wife, Nadine, being interviewed by KGU radio announcer Gene Good.

The smiling staff of Consolidated's Princess/Cinerama Theatre take a moment to pose for a picture at the premiere. The usherettes are dressed in their white uniform, which is fondly recalled by decades of island moviegoers. (Courtesy Consolidated Amusement Company.)

The 1964 world premiere of the beach party film *Ride the Wild Surf* was hosted by local radio station K-POI. The movie included real surfing footage shot in Hawai'i. The "Poi boys" were there, including "Uncle Tom" Moffett and Bob "The Beard" Lowrie, along with hundreds of enthusiastic teenage fans. (Courtesy Consolidated Amusement Company.)

The Princess was rented out in late 1964 for a national touring burlesque-style bedroom comedy starring Playboy playmate June Wilkinson. The set and plot was lacking, as were the costumes (at least for the star), but that suited the audience just fine. Wilkinson traveled the United States with this show for 15 years.

Above is the enormous Princess in its last years, alone amid the leveled acreage of the downtown urban renewal project. It was the last building demolished and the shadow of the crane with its wrecking ball can be seen on the back wall. The theatre's tall stage house enclosed a huge stage that was 45 feet deep, 45 feet wide, with a gridiron (for scenic drops) height of 82 feet from the stage floor.

A bit of dark humor appeared on the eve of the Princess demolition, as the poster case announces the last show, one that will literally "bring the house down." A small group of those who had worked on the theatre's pipe organ over the years and moved it to the Hawai'i Theatre gathered in a park facing the theatre to witness and record the sad spectacle.

The wrecking ball swings at what is left of the Princess stage house in 1969, as demolition was nearly complete, though the proscenium arch did not give up easily. In the distance is the International Theatre, at Beretania Street and Nuuanu Avenue, which today is a church.

Sailors walk towards the entrance to the Park Theatre on the edge of A'ala Park in downtown Honolulu in 1945. *Elysia* was an adult sexploitation film that had been around since 1934. Designed by Hego Fuchino for a Mr. Oda in 1919, the theatre was named Nihon-kan (Nippon Theatre) in 1925, renamed Koen Gekijo (Park Theatre) in 1934, and Nippon in 1952. It showed Asian films (except during World War II) and was demolished around 1965. (Courtesy Bishop Museum.)

The Kaimuki Playhouse as it looked in late 1927. Built by Manuel Calhau on Waialae Avenue at Wilhelmina Rise, it was designed by Hego Fuchino and opened February 10, 1922. The theatre had a Buhl and Blashfield pipe organ played by Johnny DeMello, among other organists. The ubiquitous theatre barbershop was next door. Note the advertisement for cough medicine on the roll-up awning. (Yew Char photograph. Courtesy Bishop Museum.)

The Kaimuki Playhouse was purchased by Consolidated Amusement on December 27, 1930, and renamed the Kaimuki Theatre. In the mid-1930s, it received the new facade seen in this 1940s photograph. The theatre had its own Saturday morning Porky Pig kiddie club and a loyal following of neighborhood adults. It was demolished in January 1982, and an office building took its place. (Courtesy Desoto Brown.)

The States opened in May 1922, one of five new Honolulu theatres that year. It was at the States, on Fort Street across from the Princess Theatre, that modern talking pictures were first shown in Hawai'i in 1928. Purchased by Consolidated Amuseument and closed in 1930 after only eight years, it became their film exchange. (Courtesy Hawai'i State Archives.)

The 1,300-seat Roosevelt downtown on Maunakea Street opened as the O'ahu in 1928, designed by Hego Fuchino, and was briefly known as the Uptown. Franklin Theatres purchased and renamed it in 1934 to honor President Roosevelt's Hawai'i visit that year. It became a burlesque house in the 1950s and was sold in the early 1970s, renamed the Rex and screened adult films. Acquired by the city for an affordable housing development, it was demolished in November 1985.

Here is a rare interior view of the Roosevelt stage with the footlights, also known as the curtain warmers, on. The bottom of the painted asbestos fire curtain is visible. To the left of the orchestra pit is the stage runway into the audience, used by burlesque performers. The markings were made by R. L. Grosh, a theatrical supply firm, probably in preparation for a new screen. (Courtesy Academy of Motion Picture Arts and Sciences.)

Consolidated Amusement's New Pawa'a Theatre, designed by architect Louis Davis, opened on King and Punahou Streets on January 3, 1929. That October, it and six of the company's other theatres were wired for sound. The palms on the lobby roof provided a tropical touch, but the interior decor was Mediterranean, with elaborate carved polychromed timber roof trusses. (Courtesy Hawai'i State Archives.)

The Pawaʻa was remodeled for and renamed Cinerama and opened with *The Wonderful World of the Brothers Grimm* on December 12, 1962, with actor Henry Fonda in attendance. The deeply curved screen and relatively small, raked auditorium made it an ideal place to see films. The theatre's Cinerama name and large screen survived until it closed in 1999 and was converted for retail. The stored original (and rare) Cinerama projectors were sent to Los Angeles for reuse. (Courtesy Consolidated Amusement Company.)

On the campus of Punahou School is handsome Dillingham Hall, built in 1929. It was initially designed by the New York firm of Bertram Goodhue and Associates and completed by Hardie Phillip. Its interior featured graceful exposed arches soaring above the seating for 824. In its early years, it was often used by community theatre groups. The theatre was remodeled in 1994 by architects Hardy Holzman Pfeiffer Associates. (Courtesy Punahou School Archives.)

The Mickey Mouse Club lines up in front of Hilo's Palace Theatre on September 30, 1933. At far left (with a hat) is manager Lowell Gist, and on the right (in a white suit) is organist Johnny DeMello. Designed for owner Adam Baker by Ripley and Fishbourne, surviving architects of Honolulu's Princess, the Palace opened October 25, 1925, with Douglas Fairbanks's *Don Q Son of Zorro*. Consolidated Amusement bought the theatre December 14, 1930. (Courtesy Roger Angell.)

The Young Americans Club is shown at the Palace in about 1940. Patterned after similar Saturday kiddie clubs, the Young Americans stressed patriotism, good citizenship, and community service. (Courtesy Academy of Motion Picture Arts and Sciences.)

Above is a view of the Palace interior as it looks today. It is the largest historic theatre outside Honolulu. The interior is similar in design and decor to, although smaller than, Honolulu's Princess Theatre, which is not surprising, as it was designed by the same architects three years later. Closed for many years, the Palace was saved and is now being restored through dedicated community effort. (Courtesy Historic Hawai'i Foundation.)

This photograph from around 1932 shows organist Johnny DeMello at the console of the Palace Theatre's three-manual, seven-rank Robert Morton organ. He began his long tenure as an organist and manager with Consolidated Amusement in 1928 and played at many of their theatres, including the Hilo for 10 years and the Waikiki for 23 years. He retired in 1978, ending an incredible musical career of 50 years. (Courtesy Roger Angell.)

Organist Johnny DeMello gets ready for a Mickey Mouse Club event at the Palace Theatre in 1933. Only five years after Mickey was born, the mouse was already extremely popular, and Walt Disney wisely knew the value of theatre tie-ins such as this. (Courtesy Roger Angell.)

Every member of the Palace's Mickey Mouse Club received this card on their birthday. There was also cake and ice cream for the lucky kids. The kiddie clubs provided supervised fun and games in those pre-television days (and also publicized the theatre to parents).

The Empire opened on Hilo's Haili Street on September 24, 1921, built by Adam Baker, Sr., replacing an earlier theatre of the same name around the corner on Kamehameha Avenue. Purchased by Consolidated Amusement on November 23, 1933, it closed May 25, 1940, and was converted for retail. Pictured here in 1980, it still stands today after almost 90 years. (David Franzen photograph. Courtesy State Historic Preservation Office.)

Another Hilo theatre was the Mamo, seen here in 1970. Built in 1921 as the Yuraku-Kwan (also known as Yura-Kwan), it was remodeled and renamed when the auditorium was expanded and the stage was extended to the rear of the building in 1937. In recent years, the wooden building was the home of the Hilo Community Players until the auditorium simply collapsed one day in April 1995. The remainder was subsequently demolished. (Courtesy Historic Hawai'i Foundation.)

Community residents pose in front of Minoru Taniguchi's new Olaʻa Theatre on the Big Island in 1927. A double feature, *The Show* and *Miss Nobody*, is on the bill for the evening. (M. Koga photograph. Courtesy Bishop Museum.)

The crowds lined up in 1943 at the ʻIao [ee-au] Theatre in Wailuku, Maui. Built for $40,000 in a Spanish Mission style, it opened August 22, 1928, on North Market Street and was one of several theatres in the small county seat town. It was purchased in 1993 by Maui County and restored. It is now a community performing arts venue for Maui OnStage and enjoyed by new generations of Valley Isle residents.

Four

NEIGHBORHOOD THEATRES EVERYWHERE

The introduction of modern sound films in Honolulu in 1928 at the States Theatre downtown and their resulting popularity precipitated a building boom throughout the 1930s. During this time, Consolidated Amusement built more than two dozen neighborhood and rural theatres on O'ahu and elsewhere. Every neighborhood had one, and each theatre had its loyal following. Most managers knew their regular patrons by name. Saturday morning clubs such as Mickey Mouse, Donald Duck, Popeye, Porky Pig and Buck Rogers offered fun for the kids. They had elected club officers, games, and prizes, along with free cake and ice cream on a member's birthday. Friendly competition existed among these theatres in revenue, promotional efforts, and staff social activities like bowling and softball.

Neighborhood theatres did not have the biggest screens or fancy decor (with a few exceptions), but they had a dedicated audience. Each was conveniently located and residents knew the latest films would eventually be shown there and at cheaper prices than downtown.

Consolidated Amusement operated most of Honolulu's neighborhood theatres. Its first real competition on O'ahu was Franklin Theatrical Enterprises, a small circuit that was established in 1934, later known as Royal Amusement/Royal Theatres. Franklin opened the King theatre downtown in 1935, two neighborhood theatres, the Queen (1936) and the Palace (1938), and three others later on. Consolidated had all the major studios; initially, Franklin/Royal only had Paramount and lesser majors like RKO and Republic. The company also supplied films to independent theatres operators. One unique and enviable thing Franklin/Royal did have in the 1930s was regular, albeit small, live stage shows by renowned mainland producers Fanchon and Marco.

Over the years, as population demographics shifted and the industry changed, many of these neighborhood theatres closed and were eventually demolished. The first to go in Honolulu had been open less than 20 years. Others were put to various uses, as some became churches, retail space, or warehouses. Honolulu's last freestanding neighborhood theatre, the 1939 Varsity, closed in 2007 after 68 years and was demolished the following year.

The Palama was the first of many Consolidated Amusement neighborhood theatres opened in the 1930s. Designed by architect Louis Davis in an exotic Asian style with seating for 1,100, it was built for $140,000 and opened April 19, 1930. Despite its decor, the theatre offered a mix of Hollywood and ethnic films. Leased in 1970 and renamed the Zamboanga, it featured movies from the Philippines. Sold in 1985, it was converted to retail space and now houses a church and commercial space. (Courtesy Hawai'i State Archives.)

Built in 1930, Farrington Hall at the University of Hawai'i at Manoa was the home of dramatic productions for more than 30 years. Everything from Shakespeare to Japanese Kabuki was performed on its stage. During World War II, famed actor Maurice Evans, an Army Special Services captain, directed plays there. In later years, actors often shared the stage with equally dramatic swarms of termites. The building was finally demolished in the 1960s.

Servicemen filled the beautiful Waipahu Theatre throughout World War II, as it was close to many military installations and units surrounding Pearl Harbor. (Courtesy Hawai'i State Archives.)

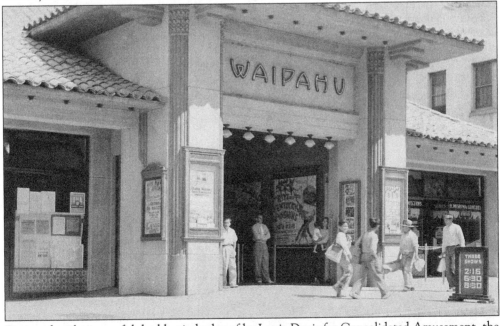

Designed with a graceful double-pitched roof by Louis Davis for Consolidated Amusement, the Waipahu Theatre opened December 21, 1930, on Depot Road, directly across from the Waipahu Sugar Mill. The year it opened ended up being Consolidated's most profitable since its founding, although the World War II years would be even better. The Waipahu was sold in 1970 and is now a church.

The Haleiwa opened on O'ahu's north shore in 1931, designed by Hego Fuchino. For five decades, the 900-seat theatre featured shows of all kinds. After a developer took over, things quickly soured. Unauthorized demolition began early one Saturday in September 1983. City officials, including the mayor, showed up to stop it. The partial demolition spawned the character of Captain Haleiwa, wearing tights and a cape in an attempt to save the day. It ultimately came to naught and the theatre fell to the wrecking ball, replaced by a McDonald's restaurant. (Courtesy Hawai'i State Archives.)

Franklin Theatres, Consolidated Amusement's first major competitor, built its first theatre, the King, in downtown Honolulu, designed by architect Herbert Cayton. The theatre opened May 22, 1935, with Republic's *Cappy Ricks Returns* and Fanchon and Marco's Sunkist Beauties on stage. It billed itself as a family theatre with films and stage shows at low admission prices.

After Franklin was acquired by Royal Theatres, the King's moderne facade was remodeled into a much blander exterior, painted dark brown, as seen in this 1950s photograph. It was later twinned and continued to show B-pictures and second-run films until it closed in 1986. The site is now a multistory parking garage. (Courtesy Academy of Motion Picture Arts and Sciences.)

A rare view of the King interior, probably from the 1950s, when a larger CinemaScope screen was planned. The measurements were made by theatrical supply firm R. L. Grosh. The two gilded proscenium columns glow in the reflected light from the camera flash. (Courtesy Academy of Motion Picture Arts and Sciences.)

Although a small theatre chain, Franklin Theatres had signficant Hollywood connections and booked good stage shows, including appearances in the late 1930s at the King and Queen Theatres by the Sunkist Beauties and other performers of famed entertainment producers Fanchon and Marco. These were led by their brother, Rube Wolf, a popular musician and bandleader. This March 10, 1939, advertisement uses a little pidgin English for fun.

The Queen in Kaimuki was Franklin Theatrical Enterprises second theatre, designed by Lyman Bigelow, and opened June 29, 1936, with the film *Loves of a Dictator* and a stage play by the Hollywood Players, *The Milky Way*. The 850-seat theatre had a shallow stage, but nonetheless featured live productions in the 1930s. Above is a photograph of the Queen in 1943.

This rare view of the Queen interior probably dates from the 1950s, when many theatres installed larger screens for CinemaScope films. The measurements were made by theatre suppliers R. L. Grosh. Note the bottom of the raised fire curtain, with the word "asbestos," once ironically assuring patrons of safety. (Courtesy Academy of Motion Picture Arts and Sciences.)

As a popular neighborhood theatre, the Queen had a special club and matinee shows for kids. Above they are lined up to see *Tarzan* on August 19, 1951. Eventually the open outer lobby around the box office seen here was enclosed. (Courtesy Academy of Motion Picture Arts and Sciences.)

The remodeled later marquee and vertical sign illuminate the neighborhood on August 20, 1951. The Queen evolved into adult films in the 1970s and is long closed, but still graces Waialae Avenue, albeit in poor condition. The Friends of the Queen Theater group and many residents are hopeful it can again become a vibrant part of the Kaimuki community. (Courtesy Academy of Motion Picture Arts and Sciences.)

The Kapahulu, seen here about 1936, was typical of many of Consolidated's 1930s neighborhood theatres, boasting a fancy facade, such as the Spanish Baroque one seen above, but hardly any ornamentation inside. The theatre opened on Kapahulu Avenue near Campbell Avenue February 21, 1936, and showed mainly second-run films, and in later years, often featured Japanese movies. Demolished in April 1980, a small strip mall is on the site. (Courtesy Theatre Historical Society of America.)

The marquee is lit up for the crowds attending an evening show at the Liliha in the 1930s. The theatre, which opened June 5, 1936, on Liliha Street near School Street, was a popular neighborhood show house for more than 25 years. The city had acquired it in 1957 for construction of the H-1 freeway, but it continued on a month-to-month basis until closing in July 1962. (Courtesy Consolidated Amusement Company.)

The Wahiawa was another of Consolidated Amusement's rural theatres of the 1930s and opened June 22, 1935, on California Avenue. It served not only residents of the area, many of whom worked in the surrounding pineapple fields, but the thousands of servicemen from nearby Schofield Barracks and Wheeler Field.

Consolidated's Kewalo opened November 5, 1937, on Cooke and Queen Streets in what was then a residential district near downtown Honolulu. The decor was in a nautical motif that featured fish, mermaids, and King Neptune. In time, the area became commercial and light industrial, and the theatre closed March 31, 1957. It was used as a film exchange for many years and is now retail space. (Courtesy Academy of Motion Picture Arts and Sciences.)

When the Palace Theatre opened November 9, 1938, at Beretania and Ke'eaumoku Streets in Honolulu's Makiki district, it was Franklin (later Royal) Theatres' third movie house in Honolulu. Renamed the Nippon in January 1965, it was subsequently twinned and eventually became the Asian Cinema Center before being demolished in the mid-1980s to make room for a gas station. The theatre is seen here in 1942 when it was selling war bonds, as noted on the marquee.

This rare photograph, probably from the time it opened, shows the striking moderne interior of the Palace, with a unique proscenium of glass blocks, lighted from behind, and aluminum-leafed murals on the auditorium walls. The later installation of a CinemaScope screen hid the proscenium, and the walls were completely draped. (Courtesy Academy of Motion Picture Arts and Sciences.)

Consolidated opened the 1,000-seat Toyo on June 16, 1938, to showcase Japanese films for the large resident population. Designed by architect C. W. Dickey, whose Waikiki Theatre opened two years earlier, its design was based on Japan's Ieayasu Shrine of the Tokugawa Shogunate. Dickey used the same concept of a large area between the street and the entrance, this time with walkways flanking a landscaped pond filled with colorful koi (carp).

The Toyo's dual walkways led to a large covered lanai beneath a curved roof and a panel depicting the three monkeys (hear no evil, see no evil, speak no evil) with a freestanding box office in a quasi-Oriental motif. The spacious area was used by patrons waiting for the next show. (Courtesy State Historic Preservation Office.)

The interior of the Toyo was richly decorated in a variety of Asian motifs, some authentic, some fanciful. Designed and executed by Consolidated staff decorators Emerson Andelin and Homer Merrill, it consisted of three-dimensional cast plaster and a variety of other material on nearly every surface. The scale of the elaborate detailing is hard to judge in this photograph. (Courtesy State Historic Preservation Office.)

Here is a close-up view of two of the wall panels in the Toyo, painted on tatami, or straw, mats with brocade and velvet fabric stenciled with various designs. (Courtesy State Historic Preservation Office.)

On each side of the screen was a large mural with carved wooden inserts, crafted of distressed plywood to highlight the grain. Nearly all this decor was destroyed along with the theatre, except for a few plaster elements that were salvaged. (Courtesy State Historic Preservation Office.)

A bulldozer attacks the Toyo in March 1988, following a strong but ultimately futile effort to save it. The theatre was well located and would have made an ideal performance venue for local arts organizations. The loss of it is still felt in the community. A credit union building now occupies the site. (Courtesy Hawai'i State Archives.)

The Varsity, seen here in 1944, was Consolidated's neighborhood theatre for Manoa Valley and opened September 8, 1939. Designed by C. W. Dickey, architect of Honolulu's beautiful Waikiki and Toyo theatres, it was a restrained expression of his talents, although he did utilize covered walkways and tropical plantings. Note the conical streetlight reflectors, installed due to wartime lighting restrictions. After the war, the theatre's green and blue neon marquee served as a friendly nighttime beacon.

In the 1960s, the nearby University of Hawai'i rented the 900-seat Varsity for large lecture classes. The theatre was twinned in 1985 and showed mostly foreign and art films in later years. The large property was sold and the theatre was demolished in March 2008 after 68 years of operation. It was Honolulu's last freestanding theatre. The site is now a parking lot.

Hawai'i's military installations all had at least one theatre. With as many as 25,000 soldiers, the U.S. Army's Schofield Barracks once had five theatres. The Post Theatre (No. 1) was the largest with 1,100 seats. Shown here shortly after it opened about 1934, it is still in use. Author James Jones was stationed at Schofield before and after the Japanese attack and used it as a setting for his novel *From Here to Eternity*. Portions of the movie were filmed there.

Fort Ruger, on the slopes of Diamond Head, was established in 1909 for coastal defense. The Post Theatre, seen above after it opened in 1934, had exterior walls of thick Canec, a fiberboard made from sugar cane. During World War II, the building was painted in camouflage colors. In 1952, Honolulu Community Theatre, now Diamond Head Theatre, moved in. The building is relatively unchanged, although its days may be numbered, as a new theatre is being planned.

This 1947 photograph is of the Kilauea Theatre, located at Kilauea Military Camp, a recreational facility adjacent to Volcanoes National Park on the Island of Hawai'i. Originally built as a barracks building, the theatre opened in the 1930s and was one of the very few military-run theatres that civilians in the area could attend. It is operated today as a community theatre.

Built in 1930, the People's Theatre was operated for decades by the Tanimoto family, who ran a chain of Big Island theatres. The projection booth could be accessed directly from the living quarters on the second floor. Purchased, restored, and operated by Dr. Tawn Keeney, it still serves the community of Honoka'a, Hawai'i.

The Honomu, built in 1931, was another Big Island theatre run by the Tanimoto family and replaced an earlier theatre nearby, in the little town on the road to famed Akaka Falls. The auditorium has been demolished; only the projection booth and facade remain.

Located in the town of Hawi, on the northern tip of the Big Island, the now demolished Hawi Theatre was built around 1935 and is seen here during January 1944, when Consolidated Amusement operated it.

An evening crowd gathers around the neon-lit Kahei Theatre in Hawi in November 1940. Built and run by Koichi Sugiyama and his wife, and later, their son Sydney, the Kahei closed a few years ago, but the building still stands. (Courtesy Bishop Museum.)

The Pahala Theatre, constructed in 1936, was typical of many rural Big Island theatres. The vernacular architecture was straightforward and without adornment, inside or out, except for the facade's roofline. Long closed, the theatre was demolished a few years ago.

Seen here is the Aloha Theatre on the Big Island of Hawai'i. Built by M. Tanimoto, it opened in 1931 as the Tanimoto Theatre and was renamed sometime during the 1950s. It is now the home of the Aloha Performing Arts Company and the Aloha Café. (Courtesy Bob Alder.)

Also on the Big Island's Kona coast is the Kona Theatre, built around 1929 by Tamajiro Marumoto, whose son Masaji became a Hawai'i supreme court justice. Later owned by businessman and Hawai'i senator William "Doc" Hill and others, the theatre is currently closed. (Courtesy Bob Alder.)

Above is the Honokahua Theatre on Maui, located in what is now the Napili resort area. This March 1974 photograph shows its unique vernacular design. The theatre is long gone. (John Wright photograph. Courtesy Bishop Museum.)

Consolidated Amusement opened Kaua'i's Lihu'e Theatre October 4, 1931. It was designed by Louis Davis, who did several other theatres for them. A large wedge-shaped marquee was added later, covering the arches. The Lihu'e showed films for 40 years, but then suffered through a series of other uses. Damaged by Hurricanes 'Iwa in 1982 and Iniki in 1992, it sat neglected for several years; the auditorium was then demolished for senior citizen apartments, but the facade and lobby were restored.

Atang de la Rama, a popular singer and film actress in the Philippines for more than 40 years, performed throughout Hawai'i and the mainland. The translation of this 1936 Kaua'i handbill is "A Big Last Show / Atang de la Rama Troupe / The stars you've been hearing and talking about are now going home and bringing your well wishes to your families and friends in the Motherland / Also showing is the movie *The Cruelty of Fate*." (Translation by University of Hawai'i Center for Philippine Studies. Courtesy Desoto Brown.)

The Aloha Theatre in the little town of Hanapepe, Kaua'i, opened in 1934. Seen here around 1970, it is one of many rural theatres that dotted the small communities on the Garden Island. Though it still stands today, it is closed. (Courtesy Historic Hawai'i Foundation.)

One of several theatres on the Island of Moloka'i, the Ka Moi (translated as "the king") opened July 25, 1939, in downtown Kaunakakai (as in the famous song "The Cockeyed Mayor of Kaunakakai"). The town also had a nearby open-air theatre, the Kukui. The Ka Moi was demolished in June 1988. (Courtesy State Historic Preservation Office.)

In an ironic life-imitates-art twist on Hollywood films with floods, this was the aftermath of a real one in Kapa'a, Kaua'i in May 1940, as kids paddle past the lobby of the Roxy Theatre the year after it opened. Designed by C. W. Dickey, it survived the waters and was a popular Garden Island movie house during World War II and for decades after, only to be done in by Hurricane Iniki in 1992. (Courtesy Bishop Museum.)

Five

THE WAIKIKI THEATRE, HONOLULU'S TROPICAL JEWEL

As early as 1930, Consolidated Amusement began planning its new deluxe flagship theatre, to be built in the resort area of Waikiki. It was to be not only elegant and up-to-date, but celebrate Hawaiʻi's tropical beauty. The architect ultimately selected to design it was C. W. (Charles) Dickey, regarded as Hawaiʻi's foremost architect. Its initial design was based on a building at Chicago's moderne 1933 and 1934 A Century of Progress International Exposition, but in harmony with its island location. The final tropical moderne design featured a large garden courtyard between the street and auditorium entrance, with lush plants surrounding a large fountain. Inside past fresco murals on the walls and ceiling, the atmospheric auditorium was flanked by lush artificial plants with the proscenium in the form of a rainbow, and tall artificial coconut palms on each side.

No expense was spared in its construction and furnishings, and it opened to great acclaim on August 20, 1936. It was undeniably the most beautiful and unique theatre ever built in Hawaiʻi. A deluxe operation, its 1,353 seats were sold on a hard-ticket, all-reserved basis. Newly released films were premiered at "First Vue" sneak previews on Friday nights. One could also make standing reservations for the same seats each week, and many attended regardless of the film being shown. A corps of smartly attired usherettes, dressed in white slacks, white short-sleeved blouse, red feather lei, a red sash and the ubiquitous flashlight, escorted you to your seat.

This first-class theatre survived as a single-screen house its entire life. However, its elegance began to fade in the 1960s as the screen got larger, eventually covering the rainbow proscenium. Later, the entrance ramps were converted to valuable retail space, the forecourt fountain disappeared, followed by the entire forecourt for an enlarged concession area. Shortly after, the lifelike artificial foliage was removed and the house draped. It was a far cry from the elegant theatre that had opened in 1936.

After 66 years of operation, soaring land values, declining attendance, and industry shifts to multiplex operations spelled the end for this once-beautiful jewel; it closed in 2002 and was demolished in 2005.

Announcing the Opening
of the beautiful new
WAIKIKI THEATER
Thursday Evening, August 20, 1936

THE INAUGURATION PROGRAM WILL BE HELD IN THE TROPICAL GARDEN OF HAWAII'S NEWEST PLAYHOUSE, STARTING AT 8 P. M. TO BE FOLLOWED SHARPLY AT 9 O'CLOCK BY THE GALA PREMIERE PERFORMANCE.

RESERVATIONS FOR THE INAUGURAL MAY BE MADE BY MAIL ORDER ONLY, AND WILL BE LIMITED TO SIX SEATS FOR EACH APPLICANT. DUPLICATED ORDERS WILL BE RETURNED UNFILLED. IN FAIRNESS TO ALL AND TO PREVENT GROUPS FROM MONOPOLIZING THE CHOICE SEATS, WE ARE OBLIGED TO STRICTLY ENFORCE THIS POLICY.

LETTERS ADDRESSED TO LOWELL B. GIST, MANAGER, WAIKIKI THEATER, c/o CONSOLIDATED AMUSEMENT COMPANY, ACCOMPANIED BY CHECK OR MONEY ORDER FOR THE NUMBER OF RESERVATIONS REQUIRED, ALONG WITH STAMPED, SELF-ADDRESSED ENVELOPE, WILL BE FILLED IN THE ORDER RECEIVED. IT WILL AID MATERIALLY IF TELEPHONE NUMBERS ARE INCLUDED, SO THE PATRON MAY BE CONSULTED IN THE EVENT OF ANY CONFUSION IN ARRANGING RESERVATION REQUESTS.

SPECIAL ATTENTION!
PLEASE DO NOT JUMP THE BARRIER TO MAKE RESERVATIONS! ANY AND ALL MAIL ORDER REQUESTS POSTMARKED PRIOR TO 6 A. M. SATURDAY, AUG. 8th, WILL NOT BE FILLED, BUT RETURNED TO THE SENDER!

PREMIERE PERFORMANCE PRICES
THE THEATER SEATING ARRANGEMENT LISTS 996 SEATS AT 65 CENTS (including tax) AND 357 SEATS AT 40 CENTS. IT IS UNDERSTOOD THAT APPLICATIONS FOR 65 CENT SEATS THAT CANNOT BE FILLED WILL BE MADE IN THE 40 CENT SECTION, WITH THE DIFFERENCE IN PRICE REFUNDED.

LICENSE ON SCALPED TICKETS WILL BE REVOKED. INFORMATION ON ATTEMPTS TO SELL TICKETS FOR HIGHER THAN THE FIXED PRICE WILL BE APPRECIATED.

The hottest tickets in Honolulu in 1936 were for the grand opening on August 20th of Consolidated Amusement's new Waikiki Theatre, which had been promoted and eagerly anticipated for months. Tickets were priced at 40¢ and 65¢ and orders were limited to six per person. Needless to say, all 1,353 tickets were quickly snapped up. The evening's dedicatory program in the garden forecourt was broadcast live on KGMB radio, with announcer Webley Edwards of *Hawaii Calls* radio fame.

The sign on the coconut tree in this August 1936 photograph announces the opening of the newly completed Waikiki Theatre. Actively planned since 1933, it was located on an acre of prime property on Kalakaua Avenue, directly across the street from the posh 1927 Royal Hawaiian Hotel and a block from the ocean. In fact, the theatre's letterhead proclaimed, "On the beach at Waikiki." (Courtesy Terry Helgesen Collection, Theatre Historical Society of America.)

As Consolidated's flagship theatre, only the best A-pictures were booked at the Waikiki. 20th Century-Fox's *Under Two Flags* with Ronald Colman was considered an appropriately important film for the grand opening. The original small two-line dual readerboards were replaced in the 1950s with ones quadruple the size to better attract patrons. (Courtesy Terry Helgesen Collection, Theatre Historical Society of America.)

Designed in a unique tropical moderne style by architect C. W. Dickey, the Waikiki was set back from the street with a large garden forecourt and fountain, flanked by ramps on each side and a large covered lanai, or veranda, next to the entrance. All of this took up nearly half of the large property and was a perfect transition in Hawai'i's tropical climate from street to auditorium.

Patrons purchased their tickets at the sidewalk box office, and then entered through the ramp on the right. The garden forecourt not only served as a pleasant waiting area and a visual prelude to the beautiful lobby and auditorium beyond, it was also spacious enough to accommodate a large crowd.

One of the eight bronze plaques on the rim surrounding Waikiki's Fountain of Stars in the forecourt, inscribed with autographs of nearly 150 Hollywood stars of the 1930s from every major studio. Among the signatures visible are those of Norma Shearer, Gary Cooper, W. C. Fields, Loretta Young, Eddie Cantor, and Franchot Tone. The fountain was removed in the early 1980s and the whereabouts of these plaques is unknown.

This photograph captures the unique nighttime beauty of the theatre, enhanced by the dramatic architectural lighting. The triangular tower sign spelled out the name in red neon letters and was visible from afar in the then low-rise resort area. Floodlights highlight the facade's moderne detailing. These elements exemplified movie palace architect S. Charles Lee's view that "the show starts on the sidewalk." (Courtesy Terry Helgesen Collection, Theatre Historical Society of America.)

After waiting for the next show in the forecourt, enjoying its lush plants and fountain stocked with water lilies and exotic, multicolored carp, patrons stepped up to the lanai and the main doors. The previous show's audience exited through the ramp on the left or the side doors of the theatre. With this design, the theatre could quickly turn over for the next show. (Courtesy Terry Helgesen Collection, Theatre Historical Society of America.)

As moviegoers entered, they were greeted by the *center spot* (at right), the chief usherette dressed in a Hawaiian cape and helmet, who directed them to the left or right where usherettes showed them to their seats. This photograph looks into the floor-to-ceiling gold mirror on the back wall. The torchiere illuminated the ceiling mural, partially visible. The two wall frescos can also be seen just inside the doors. (Courtesy Terry Helgesen Collection, Theatre Historical Society of America.)

This moderne fresco was one of a pair just inside the Waikiki's doors, executed in full color by noted artist Marguerite Blasingame, and were possibly the first frescos in Hawai'i. Blasingame was primarily a sculptor, but was clearly skilled in this medium as well. These unique works were unfortunately demolished when the theatre expanded its lobby in the early 1980s. Fortunately, color photographs were professionally taken. (Courtesy Terry Helgesen Collection, Theatre Historical Society of America.)

A line drawing of the fresco-style painting on the barrel-vaulted lobby ceiling. The fine work of Consolidated Amusement staff artist Emerson Andelin, it depicts transportation in Hawai'i through the ages and shows a double-hulled canoe, sailing ship, and the 1935 then-new Pan American Clipper. Difficult to photograph fully due to its large 30-by-50-foot size, it was also extremely fragile. Efforts to salvage it prior to the theatre's demolition proved futile.

Some of the Waikiki's usherettes line up on the stairway from the ladies' lounge around 1936. Their uniform of white slacks, white blouse, red waist and shoulder sash, red feather lei, and ever-present flashlight continued in use (minus the shoulder sash) into the 1970s. Their training included memorizing the alphabet backwards in order to seat patrons easily and holding multiple sets of tickets between their fingers. (Courtesy Hawai'i State Archives.)

96

Even the Waikiki's seats were special. The chair's end standard featured hand painted hibiscus flowers. Custom designed and crafted by Heywood-Wakefield, the deluxe and expensive seats had deep innerspring cushions and heavily padded backs, were covered in tan leatherette, and featured chrome trim around the top. The seats were used for more than 40 years until they were replaced. (David Franzen photograph. Courtesy State Historic Preservation Office.)

The tropical foliage on the sidewalls, made of hand painted papier-mâché and plaster, was very realistic, even up close. Among the plants were papaya, breadfruit, bougainvillea, cactus, hala, ti, and night-blooming cereus. The artistic product of Homer Merrill, the foliage survived until the 1980s when the auditorium was draped. (Courtesy Terry Helgesen Collection, Theatre Historical Society of America.)

This 1936 photograph shows the Waikiki's atmospheric interior, with its dark blue curved ceiling, flanked by artificial, yet very realistic-looking plants, lit from below. On either side of the rainbow proscenium arch were coconut palms, made of cast concrete with papier-mâché fronds that rustled in the air-conditioned breeze. Wider movie screens first partially obscured, and later completely covered the rainbow and the palm trees, which were then removed.

When the show was about to begin, the house lights dimmed to half, then went out as the ceiling was bathed in blue and the rainbow glowed in ever-changing sunset colors. Green lights shone through the foliage along the sidewalls, as clouds moved across the night sky. The footlights illuminated the picture curtain, which parted as the opening title appeared on the screen and another show began.

The Waikiki's first musical director and organist was Edwin Sawtelle, who held the position from 1936 to 1955. The theatre opened with one of the first electric Hammond Model A organs in Hawai'i, but it was underpowered for the large auditorium. Sawtelle had the pipe organ at the Hawai'i Theatre moved to the Waikiki in 1937. The retrofitting of such a large instrument, never originally planned, was a major effort and achievement. (Courtesy Terry Helgesen Collection, Theatre Historical Society of America.)

Organist Sawtelle poses with the Waikiki Theatre Girls Chorus, a group of usherettes who performed before the film and on other special occasions, including accompanying the organ for several recordings. Having a good singing voice was a factor in being hired as an usherette. The group went by various names through the years, including the Maids o' Melody. (Courtesy Terry Helgesen Collection, Theatre Historical Society of America.)

Above is the well-equipped and spotless projection booth at the Waikiki. The equipment was the finest available and most fittings were chrome-plated. Next to the three projectors, at left, is the Brenograph projector and a follow spotlight. There was an adjacent small booth, open to the auditorium, which was used by a sound technician during live events and radio broadcasts. Only the best operators worked at the Waikiki, some for decades. (Courtesy Terry Helgesen Collection, Theatre Historical Society of America.)

Shown are the Brenkert F7 Master Brenograph, an extraordinary special effects projector, left, and the carbon arc follow spotlight. The Brenograph had a comprehensive array of filters, patterns, liquid gates, mirrors and mechanical faders, and irises that could produce an incredible variety of lighting effects. The company's slogan was "Projects everything but the picture." The F7 was the top-of-the-line model, which not all theatres could afford. (Courtesy Terry Helgesen Collection, Theatre Historical Society of America.)

The Waikiki hosted several world premieres in the 1930s of films set in Hawai'i. Bing Crosby poses in front of the theatre for his *Waikiki Wedding* premiere on March 25, 1937. Other premieres included *Hawaii Calls* with Bobby Breen on February 24, 1938, which jointly premiered at the Princess, and *Honolulu* starring Robert Young, Eleanor Powell, and Burns and Allen on February 2, 1939. (Courtesy Desoto Brown.)

A Japanese film was screened at the Waikiki for the first and possibly only time at noon on January 1, 1938. *Renai Hawai Koro* (translated as *Lovers in Hawai'i's Paradise*), reportedly the first talkie filmed outside Japan, was about a theatre owner from Hawai'i who visits Japan and included scenes shot at the Waikiki. Efforts to locate this Nikkatsu film have been unsuccessful and it is apparently lost. (Courtesy Academy of Motion Picture Arts and Sciences.)

Dorothy Lamour was one of many Hollywood stars that regularly vacationed in Hawai'i. She sailed to the Islands on Matson's luxury liner *Matsonia* for the world premiere of her film, *Typhoon*, on April 25, 1940. She appeared again two days later and was the special guest on *Hawaii Calls*, the famed radio program, broadcast live from the Waikiki's courtyard.

Week Starting
First-Vue, Friday, August 16, 1940

1
PARAMOUNT NEWS
The Eyes and Ears of the World

2
POPULAR SCIENCE
Our Modern World

3
SNUBBED BY A SNOB
Color Classic

4
EDWIN SAWTELLE
Presents
THE WELCOME-ETTES
In
LAHANAU HOOKAULANA
(Anniversary Entertainment)
(a) Honolulu...................Opening Ensemble
(Written and arranged By Edwin Sawtelle)
(b) Modern Hulas.................Beatrice King
(Malihini Melody..........by Edwin Sawtelle)
(Lovely Hula Hands.........by Alex Anderson)
Solo by Lolita Kahele
(c) Songs Old and New................Medley
(d) Ancient Hulas....................Dance Trio
(Liliu E) — (Kila Kila O Maui)
(e) Finale.......................Entire Company

The Welcome-ettes

Vocal Trio	Jeanette Camara, Lolita Kahele, Betty King
Solo Dancer	Beatrice King
Dance Trio	Helen Boozer, Molly Cutter, Vivian Silva
Orchestral Trio	Val Ridge, Shigeru Ohye, Kunio Miyazono
Ensemble	Marion Arnold, Elsie Brown, Ethlye Johnson, Lolita Kahele, Charlotte Kellette, Jane Gomes, Frances Landgraf, Frances Norton, Betty King, Jeanette Camara, Mildred Aflague, Pearl Downing.

Production under direction of Edwin Sawtelle
Dances under direction of Marguerite Lee

5
MY LOVE CAME BACK
The Cast

Amelia Cornell	Olivia de Havilland
Tony Baldwin	Jeffrey Lynn
Dusty Rhodes	Eddie Albert
Joy O'Keefe	Jane Wyman
Julius Malette	Charles Winninger
Mrs. Malette	Spring Byington
Dr. Kobbe	Grant Mitchell
Paul Malette	William Orr
Valerie Malette	Ann Gillis
Geza Peyer	S. Z. Sakall
Dr. Downey	Charles Trowbridge
Dowager	Mabel Taliaferro
Agent	William Davidson
Sophie	Nanette Vallon
Butler	Sidney Bracy

6
Exit March.......................Waikiki Parade

The Waikiki's Fourth Anniversary program for the week of August 16, 1940, presented a complete and varied array of music, dance, and film. The Welcome-ettes doubled as the theatre usherettes and performed with musical director and organist Edwin Sawtelle. They were also known as the Waikiki Girls Chorus and several other names through the years. (Courtesy Desoto Brown.)

Standing in front of the gates or by the forecourt fountain were popular places for having your picture taken in Waikiki and countless visitors did it. This lone and anonymous sailor, photographed in May 1944, was one of a half-million servicemen who passed through Hawai'i during World War II. Seeing the latest Hollywood film at the Waikiki was a pleasant and inexpensive way to spend a few off-duty hours.

Servicemen fill the sidewalk in front of the theatre in 1944. Some stroll along while others stand in line to see Betty Grable's latest picture. The Royal Hawaiian Hotel across the street had been taken over by the U.S. Navy as a recreation center for submarine crews, who paid very little for rooms once occupied by wealthy tourists. They enjoyed relaxing on the beach, in spite of the barbed wire still in place.

The war was still on—Victory over Japan Day was still a month away—when these two tickets went unused. From its opening in 1936 well into the 1950s, the Waikiki was a reserved seat, hard-ticket theatre, offering two shows daily. Standing reservations could be made for the same seats each week, and many did so, often attending without knowing what movie was playing.

The two large wraparound marquee readerboards look out over a relatively quiet Kalakaua Avenue, still lined with tall palm trees in this 1952 photograph, when Hawai'i had a mere 60,000 visitors. Statehood, along with the many high-rises that would replace the palms, was still seven years away. Today more than 100 times as many visitors—6 million plus—come to Hawai'i every year.

Organist Johnny DeMello entertained thousands of moviegoers in his 23 years at the console of the Waikiki pipe organ from 1955 until 1978. He was known for the array of colorful Aloha-print jackets he wore. He once said, "They only see my back so I want to give them something to look at."

Bob Alder took over the Waikiki console in 1980 from Frank Loney, who followed DeMello for two years starting in 1978. A talented musician, Bob entertained Waikiki audiences for 17 years from 1980 to 1997, before moving to Hilo and becoming actively involved in restoring the Palace Theatre. When he departed, the organ had been played regularly for an incredible 60 years at the Waikiki and 15 years before that at the Hawai'i Theatre. (Courtesy Bob Alder.)

By the 1990s, the Waikiki had only a vestige of its former grandeur. Outside, shops replaced the dual access ramps and the garden forecourt and fountain were eliminated when the lobby was extended. Inside, the moderne murals were eliminated, as was the outside lanai; a large cafeteria-style concession was installed in its place. In the auditorium, the tropical foliage was replaced by drapery. Only the upper exterior facade remained untouched.

Although greatly altered in its final 20 years, the demolition in April 2005 of the once-elegant Waikiki, Hawai'i's most unique and beautiful theatre, is still lamented by many as an outstanding example of Hawaiian regional architecture, as well as by those who fondly remember attending movies in this once-grand showplace.

Six

Hawai'i at War and Afterwards

The early 1940s saw little new theatre construction. On the Island of Hawai'i, the Hilo, designed by C. W. Dickey for Consolidated Amusement, opened in April 1940. Built only a few yards from Hilo Bay, it was struck by two tsunamis in 1946 and again in 1960, after which it never reopened

Consolidated also built the Kohala, in the northern part of the island, which opened in August 1940. Also designed by Dickey, it was a simple, yet tasteful shingled wooden structure surrounded by hundreds of acres of sugar cane and little else. Long closed and derelict, the auditorium collapsed around 1995.

In Honolulu, the Kuhio in Waikiki was almost finished and about to open when Pearl Harbor was attacked. The U.S. Navy leased the unfinished building during World War II as an air-conditioned warehouse. It was finally returned, completed, and opened in June 1945.

Hastily constructed or converted theatres (including outdoor theatres) served the many military bases by entertaining the influx of more than 500,000 servicemen. This also provided brisk business for local theatres in spite of evening curfew restrictions. At first, shows in town had to be out by dusk; this curfew was later extended to 9:00 p.m.

Postwar theatre construction was also sparse. Hawai'i's first drive-in theatre, originally known simply as The Drive-In, opened in August 1949 for 750 cars on a large parcel of land just outside Waikiki. Closed in 1962, the area is now a crowded complex of residential condominiums, office buildings, and stores.

The Hilo Theatre, on the Island of Hawai'i, is pictured under construction in 1940. Designed by C. W. Dickey, it was built next to Hilo Bay, as seen in this Hilo Flying Service photograph. That proved to be an unfortunate location, as it was struck by two tsunamis in 1946 and 1960. After the last one, it was not reopened. (Courtesy Academy of Motion Picture Arts and Sciences.)

Consolidated Amusement's Hilo Theatre opened on April 26, 1940, and was the first modern theatre in Hilo. The three-manual, seven-rank Robert Morton pipe organ was moved over from the Palace Theatre and played regularly by Johnny DeMello before shows. (Courtesy Roger Angell.)

A beautiful night view of the Hilo, taken shortly after it opened. It was a landmark along Kamehameha Avenue for 20 years until destroyed by Mother Nature. (Courtesy Roger Angell.)

Architect Dickey again utilized the design element of covered walkways flanked with tropical plants leading to the outside lobby, box office and theatre entrance. In all, Dickey designed five theatres for Consolidated Amusement: the Waikiki, Toyo, Varsity, Kohala, and Hilo, and one independently owned theatre, the Roxy on Kaua'i. (Courtesy Roger Angell.)

The spacious auditorium of the 1,100-seat Hilo was almost completely devoid of decoration, as was fairly typical of theatres built during this time. Dickey's Varsity Theatre in Honolulu, opened the year before, had a similar plain interior. (Courtesy Roger Angell.)

The attractive usherettes of the new Hilo Theatre are pictured above in an inaugural publication. They are, from top to bottom, (left) chief usherette Alice S. H. Lau, Winona Mew Yung Yap, and Gladys Kum Hung Chow; (right) assistant chief usherette Gladys Kam Yee Mark, Ah Mai Lee, and Gladys En Yin Ching.

Organist Johnny DeMello, seen here with announcer Ken McAlister, presented regular broadcasts on KHBC radio. The organ console was destroyed by the 1960 tsunami, which crashed through the rear of the theatre and out the front; pieces were found hundreds of yards away. The surviving pipe work was purchased by Roger Angell and reinstalled in his family home in Honolulu. The organ was later donated back to the Palace Theatre. (Courtesy Roger Angell.)

This snapshot shows some of the debris from the 1960 tsunami littering the parking lot next to the Hilo Theatre. After the last tsunami, no buildings were allowed along the waterfront on Kamehameha Avenue. Today the entire area is a park.

The abandoned Kohala Theatre stands in Kapaʻau on the Big Island. Designed by C. W. Dickey for Consolidated Amusement, it opened August 30, 1940. Although in a small plantation community surrounded by acres of sugar cane fields, its large neon signs reading "KOHALA" could be seen for miles around. Closed for many years, with the seats and floor removed and back wall opened up, it was used as a warehouse and stable. Vines grew through the walls and the auditorium eventually collapsed.

Although only a small Maui town, Paʻia, or Lower Paʻia, had three theatres in the 1930s: the Lower Paʻia, also known as the Narumaru; the Paʻia; and the Princess. This is the New Princess, built in 1940 on Baldwin Avenue, as it looked in 1966. Operated by Mamoru Takitani, the exterior and roof were of corrugated metal. The Princess is long gone, as are the other theatres there.

Located behind the Toyo Theatre downtown on Aʻala Street, the Kokusai (translated as "international") Theatre opened May 7, 1941, designed by Hego Fuchino. During World War II, it was renamed the International and screened Hollywood films. It operated until late 1963; the following year, the theatre reopened in a new location at Beretania Street and Nuuanu Avenue.

Air raid alerts were still a fact of life during wartime Honolulu in May 1944. Projectionists had an assortment of glass slides ready to be shown for the drills or various other situations, such as ordering military units or fire station crews to report for duty. One odd slide reminded evening patrons who parked on the street that their car taillights had to be lit to avoid being ticketed.

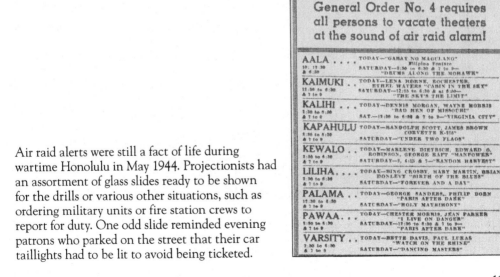

Office workers, shoppers, and children crowd the sidewalk alongside traffic going up Fort Street past the Princess Theatre during an air raid evacuation drill of downtown Honolulu on November 4, 1943. The movie playing, coincidentally, was *Flight for Freedom*. Hawai'i had been under strict martial law for almost two years and it would be almost another year until it was lifted. (HWRD1168. Courtesy Hawai'i War Records Depository, University of Hawai'i Library.)

The enormous influx of servicemen necessitated the building of theatres on or near the many new military installations. The open-air Ghormley Theatre (named for Vice Admiral Robert L. Ghormley, Commandant of the 14th Naval District in Hawai'i) was located near Pearl Harbor. (HWRD2086. Courtesy Hawai'i War Records Depository, University of Hawai'i Library.)

A U.S. Navy band at the Ghormley Theatre waits to play while they, along with an audience of sailors, listen as an officer speaks. Judging by the wooden supports on the palm tree to the right, the theatre was probably newly completed. (Tai Sing Loo photograph. Courtesy Bishop Museum.)

Veteran showbiz troopers Bob Hope and Jerry Colonna were among many famous stars that performed for servicemen in Hawai'i during the war, while on their way to entertain troops in the Pacific. This was taken during a stop at Schofield Barracks. (HWRD1380. Courtesy Hawai'i War Records Depository, University of Hawai'i Library.)

Numerous recreational facilities were operated by the military or USO in Hawai'i. The Hale Ki'i Oni Oni (House of Movies) was among them, possibly on the Waianae coast, judging by the kiawe trees. Both movies are from 1944. (Courtesy Desoto Brown.)

This 1960s photograph shows the Ford Island Theatre at Naval Air Station, Pearl Harbor, built around early 1944. Its basement also doubled as a bomb shelter. After some years of disuse, it was refurbished as a conference center, located close to two historic battleships, the USS *Arizona* and USS *Missouri*, and the Pacific Aviation Museum. (Courtesy U.S. Navy.)

In 1941, Consolidated Amusement built a second theatre in Waikiki, the Kuhio, named after Hawai'i's delegate to Congress, Prince Jonah Kuhio. Designed by San Francisco architect Vincent Raney, it was ready to open in early 1942, but following the attack on Pearl Harbor, it was leased by the U.S. Navy for air-conditioned storage and office space.

This view was taken shortly after the Kuhio opened on June 21, 1945, with *A Song to Remember*. The auditorium, with recessed ceiling cove lighting, featured black-lighted murals of tropical flowers on the sidewalls, flanked by softly lit torchieres shaped like Hawaiian kahili, and fluorescent aisle carpeting that glowed in the dark. The Kuhio, later twinned and draped, finally closed November 30, 1995, and was demolished in January 1996 for retail development.

The Kuhio's lobby lounge had floor-to-ceiling mirrors, a large glass block wall, and upholstered moderne tubular steel furniture. On one side of the lounge was a tiny phone booth whose door had a narrow, vertical glass window etched with the word "telephone" in an art deco typeface.

An attractive focal point of the Kuhio's lobby was the water fountain. Enclosed by wrap-around glass blocks lighted from behind, the stainless steel fountain was both unique and beautiful. It almost made you want to drink from it.

This view of the ladies' lounge of the Kuhio shows the moderne upholstered chairs lining the make-up table and mirrors. Tall glass block windows provided light by day, and the formed copper soffit provided indirect light in the evening.

The elaborate and spectacular exterior neon lighting of the Kuhio Theatre is shown in all its glory in 1945. Neon was not only on the walls and vertical sign, but also under the lobby canopy. On the tower, the sign spelled out "K-U-H-I-O," then the circles lit up successively, ending with the starburst at the top. This amazing neon display was certainly the most unique in Honolulu.

Seen here, at the Kuhio's invitational premiere of *The Sound of Music* on March 30, 1965, are Hawai'i governor John Burns (with a rare smile) and Kailua resident Hedwig von Trapp, whose family was portrayed in the film. Von Trapp, wearing her Austrian dirndl dress as she did everyday, taught at parochial school in Hawai'i for many years and directed a children's choir. The film played for a record 81 weeks. (Courtesy Consolidated Amusement Company.)

The invitational premiere of the movie *Hawaii* on October 17, 1966, was a gala event at the Kuhio, attended by government and business leaders and several of the film's stars. Reaction to the movie was mixed but generally positive. The book's prolific author, James Michener, is also known in Hawai'i for his collection of more than 5,000 Japanese prints donated to the Honolulu Academy of Arts. (Courtesy Consolidated Amusement Company.)

Shown here from a theatre trade publication are renderings of two of the five new theatres Consolidated Amusement planned in 1945 but never built. Above is the 1,500-seat Lelani [sic], intended for a downtown site at King and Richards Streets, across from 'Iolani Palace. Below is the 1,200-seat Alapa'i, planned for property at Alapa'i, Lunalilo, and Lusitana Streets at the edge of downtown. Designed by architect Vincent Raney, they would have been attractive, modern theatres, much like his Kuhio in Waikiki.

The U.S. Army's Fort Shafter Theatre opened on May 12, 1948, seating 995. The work of Cole McFarlane, former design chief of the Honolulu District Engineers, the building cost more than $800,000 in non-appropriated funds. The open-air walkways and entrance are similar to that of the Varsity Theatre and well suited to the climate. Renamed Richardson Theatre around 1954, it is now the home of the Army Community Theatre.

Hawai'i's first drive-in opened at 1620 Kapi'olani Boulevard on August 14, 1949, with *I Wake Up Screaming.* At first called simply The Drive-In, it was renamed Kapi'olani Drive-In when others opened. The 750-car drive-in closed April 29, 1962, and the 29 acres of prime real estate were redeveloped into a dense complex of high-rise office buildings and condominiums.

Seven

INNOVATION AND THE LAST HURRAH

New theatre construction was sparse in the 1950s. Owners concentrated on the latest innovations, such as 3-D, CinemaScope, and stereophonic sound, to compete with television. Ironically, Consolidated Amusement owned a major stake in Hawaiian Broadcasting System Ltd., which went on the air with Honolulu's first television station, KGMB, in December 1952.

The first of many Consolidated closings began in 1957, when three neighborhood theatres were sold or converted to other uses—the Kalihi, Kewalo and Liliha.

As the 1950s ended, Consolidated itself was sold three times in succession, first to a developer who sold off much of its valuable real estate, then to a Seattle businessman. He then turned around and sold the chain in 1959 to William Forman and his Pacific Theatres, who already owned a majority stake in Royal Theatres.

The 1960s saw two new Consolidated drive-ins, the Kam (short for Kamehameha) in 1962, and the Kailua in 1965; both are now closed.

Two new theatres for Japanese films were built in Honolulu. The Toho at 1646 Kapiʻolani Boulevard opened on July 2, 1964, became Consolidated's Kapiʻolani in 1976 showing films of all types, and was converted for retail in 1988. The International opened October 15, 1964, at Beretania Street and Nuʻuanu Avenue, then became the Empress showing Chinese films, closed in 1973, and is now a church. The popularity of these ethnic theatres was brief, largely replaced by such movies on videotape and television.

In October 1964, the elegant Royal opened—the first new theatre in Waikiki since World War II. The flagship (and first Waikiki operation) of Royal Theatres, its contemporary design featured outdoor fountains and a spacious interior seating 900, but it lasted less than two decades. The Royal chain was eventually sold and its theatres were ultimately sold or demolished.

The decade of the 1960s was the last hurrah for single-screen theatres. Consolidated's two adjacent 900-seat giants, Waikiki 1 and 2, opened in 1970. Soon after, the multiplexing and shopping-mall theatres began and, one by one, most freestanding theatres closed and fell. In 2008, Honolulu's last operating neighborhood movie theatre, the Varsity, was demolished after 68 years, and with it went the end of an era.

FOR THE FIRST TIME IN HONOLULU!
THE WORLD'S FIRST
FEATURE LENGTH
MOTION PICTURE
IN
3 DIMENSION

Arch Oboler Master of the Unusual, presents

BWANA DEVIL

ROBERT STACK
BARBARA BRITTON
NIGEL BRUCE
Released thru United Artists

A LION in your lap!

A LOVER in your arms!

NOT SHORT SUBJECTS...BUT A REAL FEATURE...AND IN COLOR, TOO!

OPENS SUNDAY

LIBERTY *Theatre*
PHONE 57060—1175 NUUANU AVE.

CONTINUOUS PERFORMANCES
SUNDAY: FROM 12:30 P.M.
DAILY: FROM 11 A.M.
ALL SHOWS UNRESERVED
ADULTS $1.10—CHILDREN 55¢
(Tax Included)

NOTE—Liberty Theater will be closed today and tomorrow so that SPECIAL 3-DIMENSION EQUIPMENT may be installed! SUNDAY is the BIG OPENING DAY of "BWANA DEVIL"

The 1950s were a difficult time for theatres everywhere because of the popularity of television. To lure patrons back, they installed wider screens for the new CinemaScope features, and showed 3-D movies. The golden age of 3-D began in 1952 with the *Bwana Devil*, shown locally at the Liberty Theatre beginning May 17, 1953.

The Kaiser Dome at the Hawaiian Village Hotel, which was built of Kaiser aluminum, was erected in just 22 hours during January 1957. Licensed from Buckminster Fuller, Kaiser and showman Mike Todd planned to market them for theatrical use. Todd's blockbuster film *Around the World in 80 Days* opened there on the first of November, with Todd and then-wife Elizabeth Taylor in attendance. Four months later, Todd died in a plane crash. The 2,000-seat dome hosted everything from symphony concerts to surfing films until demolished in 1999 for a hotel tower. (Courtesy Desoto Brown.)

In the early 1960s, famed architect I. M. Pei designed three buildings for the new East-West Center in Honolulu, including this striking 630-seat theatre that could accommodate both Asian and Western staging. Shortly before its 1963 opening, President Kennedy was assassinated and it was named in his honor. During Kennedy Theatre's first two seasons as home of University of Hawai'i theatre productions, then-UH student Bette Midler appeared in several plays. (Bob Chinn photograph. Courtesy University of Hawai'i.)

The new Royal Theatre at 2380 Kuhio Avenue was built for $700,000 as Royal Theatres flagship and their first Waikiki venture. Designed by local architects Wimberly, Whisenand, Allison, and Tong, it opened October 15, 1964, with *Becket*. The elegant, 872-seat single-screen theatre's life was brief, as it was demolished in 1982, replaced by an open-air restaurant. Over the years, there have been eight movie theatres in Waikiki; sadly, none of them remain today.

Honolulu's municipal theatre–concert hall opened September 13, 1964, after decades of planning. Designed by William Merrill, of Merrill, Simms, and Roehrig, and built on the former Ward estate known as Old Plantation, across from Thomas Square, the modern 2,158-seat facility opened with a black-tie Honolulu Symphony concert under conductor George Barati. Originally called Honolulu International Center, with the unfortunate acronym HIC, the complex was renamed for Mayor Neal Blaisdell, who championed its completion. (Courtesy Hawai'i State Archives.)

Hawai'i has enjoyed a fascinating variety of theatres in the last century and a quarter. Some have been like their mainland counterparts; others are unique to the islands and its climate, people, or lifestyle. This admission sign, found in a Big Island rural movie theatre, typifies something found only in Hawai'i. (Haole is the Hawaiian term for Caucasian.) And this is as good a way as any to end this look at Hawai'i's theatres.

INDEX

Visit us at
arcadiapublishing.com

CPSIA information can be obtained
at www.ICGtesting.com
Printed in the USA
LVOW02*1528050917
547613LV00025B/695/P